Quit Smoking in One Day

Quit Smoking in One Day

Jan Geurtz

Ambo | Amsterdam

Also by Jan Geurtz

De verslaving voorbij
Het einde van de opvoeding
Verslaafd aan liefde
Verslaafd aan denken

ISBN 978 90 263 2793 3

The first edition was published in 2010 by F.Y.I Media Group
Translated by Mimi Visser
Original title *De opluchting. In één dag van het roken af*
Cover design Studio Jan de Boer
Cover illustration Tony Stone

Contents

Preface

Every smoker has heard one or two of those tall tales. There's the uncle who smokes like a chimney for twenty years. One fine day he extinguishes his thirtieth cigarette and tells his wife, "I quit." He never smoked again after that day and has never been bothered by it.

Secretly, every smoker hopes that one day he will have a moment of enlightenment that will free him from smoking for good. But with most smokers, this is not the case. I quit smoking after I had an intensive encounter session with the Essence organization in Holland. This training brings you face to face with your emotional blocks and hands you a method to let go of them. Addiction (to smoking) is an extreme form of an emotional block. The intellect says for a long time that it's better to quit, but the emotions are a battleground of fear and longing, pride and shame, responsibility and guilt. The breaking of this emotional block is the most important step a smoker has to take in order to be able to quit smoking successfully and without problems.

In the Free Yourself Method, some elements of the views of Allen Carr are used as inspiration for a totally new rational-emotive method to free oneself from smoking in a short period of time. All the practical examples in this book come from Free Yourself seminars that I have given since January 1997, in which participants free themselves from smoking in a single day.

I extend my warmest feelings of gratitude to Michal Perl for her support and friendship during the development of the Free Yourself Method. The same is valid for Mickey van Gendt, with whom I had the very first talks about the Free Yourself Method. A lot of support was given to me by Harriet Tax, who quit smoking with me and assisted me when I gave the first Free Yourself Method training sessions. For the American Edition I am very gratefull to Mimi Visser in New York who voluntarily translated the Dutch version into English after it had helped her to quit smoking. Finally, I'm very grateful to myself for ending this exceptionally destructive smoke addiction. By succeeding in that, my life has become a lot more fun.

Introduction

"How could reading a book ever free me from smoking?" is a question you may have asked upon seeing this book. And you would have a point there, because this book cannot free you from smoking. No book, no method, no nicotine patch, chewing gum, or laser beam can do that. The simple, inevitable truth about quitting smoking is that you have to do it all by yourself.

But how?

There is a hard way and there is an easy way. The hard way is well known to almost every smoker. It's the way of fighting yourself and your constant obsession with smoking for weeks, if not months. This book shows you the easy way.

All those fears that come up when you think of quitting smoking—the withdrawal symptoms, the obsessive yearning for a cigarette, the depression, the sheer emptiness of a life without smoking—none of this will appear to be true. Smoking is like a nightmare from which you will wake up, and from the first smoke-free day, it will be a great relief. You will hardly have withdrawal symptoms, so you won't feel the urge to eat more snacks. In fact, with this method you will gain little if any weight at all. Quitting smoking will appear to be exactly the opposite of what you were always afraid it would be. You will find that it's fun to quit, that it feels great to be freed from this compulsion to smoke, and that it's fantastic to feel fit and energetic.

The ambiguous feelings that accompany the smoking of every cigarette—the feeling of doing something you actually don't agree with, sometimes lighting a cigarette when you don't even want to, the feeling that you seem to give yourself a little treat with a cigarette while your lungs and body know that you are ruining yourself, this ambiguousness, this discontentment with yourself, this dependence—all this misery can be disposed of in one day! This book tells you how.

But you will have to read it the right way.

Chapter 1

How Should You Read This Book?

Here are some instructions that you'll have to keep in mind in order to successfully quit smoking with this book. The first one is:

1. Keep smoking while you are reading and try to enjoy it.

This means that you shouldn't try to smoke a little less as a precursor to quitting. Smoking less is much harder than quitting. Moreover, it doesn't make sense, because there is no such thing as "becoming less addicted." By trying to smoke less, all you do is increase the fear of quitting—and by doing so, you strengthen the addiction.

It also means that you shouldn't deliberately smoke more. I have heard of people who tried to help themselves in that way: to smoke so much that it makes them sick, after which it becomes easier to quit. This also doesn't work. You've already known for a long time that smoking is bad for you and that it makes you sick. By smoking more than you usually do, you only enhance your dependence.

This first instruction also says: Try to enjoy it. What I mean is, smoke as consciously as possible and if you like it, enjoy it. If you don't like it, don't feel guilty but think, "Soon I will be freed from this forever."

Try to stop feeling stupid or weak or guilty about your smoking. While reading this book allow yourself to smoke, maybe for the first time in your life. Really smoke because that's the best way of being freed from it in the near future, forever.

2. Don't skip anything. Read every chapter only after you have read the previous one.

Some people are so curious about the outcome of this book that they sneak a look at the last page right away. If you do that, you'll miss the point. You won't find one page somewhere in the back of this book that will free you from smoking. The flow of the chapters will gradually break your dependence on smoking. Read this book from A to Z.

Others start looking right away for the passage that allows them to say, "See, it's a worthless method!" If you want to prove that it's not possible to quit smoking the easy way, you'll undoubtedly succeed. In that case, you can spare yourself the trouble of reading on (and of quitting smoking). Of course, it will be a pity that you will never know why so many other people have quit so easily. So what do you want: to confirm your own prejudice, or to quit smoking the easy way? Well, then!

3. Read the book in as short a period of time as possible.

Some readers of this book will feel after reading some chapters, "Gee, this is a good book. What if it really makes me quit?" And they will start reading more and more slowly. Smokers are experts in fooling themselves, in thinking one thing and doing the other. By reading this book, we feel as if we are quitting, and we use that to repress the feelings of guilt we have about the fact that we're not quitting. In reality, these slow readers are victims of their own fear. But don't worry, this book doesn't take anything from you; it doesn't force you in any way to quit smoking. You don't HAVE to quit smoking when you have finished this book. The decision of quitting or not quitting—and when—is for you to make. It's the smoking that you often do against your will, never the quitting. However, there is a big possibility that you will feel very strongly like quitting smoking when you've finished reading this book.

This third instruction comes down to reading every chapter before you have forgotten the previous one.

Some smokers will gradually build their decision to quit while reading this book. My advice to them is to read at least one chapter every day. Reading even slower is fooling yourself. The more chapters you read in a day, the better.

Do you want to free yourself from smoking as soon as possible? Then the best way is to take an afternoon and an evening to read the book all at once. Take a break of an hour once in a while, to eat or to take a walk—to be alone with yourself. Turn off your cell phone and make this day a special adventure—a gift from you to yourself. You'll never regret it.

Chapter 2

Is Quitting Smoking Hard or Easy?

Every smoker will answer this question with "Quitting smoking is very, very hard." Every ex-smoker who quit using the Free Yourself Method will say, "It was actually quite easy." Here are some reactions of ex-smokers who quit using the Free Yourself Method.

"I haven't smoked since the training, and I totally don't miss it. I'm not repelled by it; I'm not attracted. Actually I feel nothing about smoking at all." (Jane, 42, journalist)

"I was a little skeptical after the Free Yourself training. But the next day I noticed right away: It really works! I haven't had any trouble." (Ben, 63, musician)

"Even with a glass of wine, I don't need a cigarette anymore. I'm so happy! And it's so nice to have time to think of other things than cigarettes." (Sara, 32, mother of two children)

"After the movies, in a bar with a beer and some friends around me that smoke, I don't need a cigarette anymore." (Martin, 24, student)

"I realize that I should never start smoking again. But it's a good feeling to know that I also don't have to anymore!" (Tom, 36, shipbuilder)

How is it possible that so many ex-smokers say that it was easy to quit, while you, future ex-smoker, are convinced that it will be a terribly difficult undertaking? Who is the crazy one here, the smoker or the ex-smoker? The answer is: neither of them. Quitting is hard and it's easy, depending on the way you do it. I'll give an example for clarification.

Some time ago, I was in an old parsonage, rehearsing with an amateur choir to which I belong. (BTW, my singing is much better since I quit smoking!) When I tried to leave the premises, I was prevented from doing so by a beautiful old wooden door with a lot of brassware that wouldn't open. There was not a millimeter of movement in the handle. I searched among all the brassware, to see if there was a little peg, bolt, or other mechanism that could be the reason that the handle wouldn't move. There was nothing of the sort. Then I tested the hypothesis that the handle was jammed and pushed it with all my might. I wasn't able to confirm or dismiss this hypothesis, because if the handle was jammed, my strength wasn't sufficient to force it open, and if there was another way of opening the door, I couldn't find it. My imagination wandered in the direction of chain saws, and not knowing what to do next I looked around a little. My eye fell on a little piece of cardboard that was next to the door on the floor, a little card with a message on it. I picked it up and read: HANDLE UP. This little piece of cardboard had clearly been glued to the door and contained crucial information for opening this monumental door in an easy way: by pulling the handle up instead of pushing it down. I left the place chuckling.

Was it hard to open this door or was it easy? Without the right information, it was definitely very hard, almost impossible. With the right information, it was ridiculously easy. The easiest way in all other cases—to push the handle down—was in this case a very hard way. In other words: you'll find the easy way by doing exactly the opposite of what you always have been taught to do.

In the same way, you could see quitting smoking as something very hard, or as something very simple, depending on the method that you use. The simple way is found by thinking in the opposite direction of what you would normally expect. Every smoker thinks of quitting in terms of willpower, discipline, and perseverance. The simple method chooses the opposite approach. You will do more than just chuckle, when you leave the prison of smoking through this door and experience the freedom of the open air.

Chapter 3

Free in Just One Day? How Is that Possible?

For most smokers, it is a bewildering thought that something that you do for so many years, day after day, could be finished in one day. After all, smoking is something that you're terribly dependent on, that you're sometimes ashamed of, that you have wanted to quit for so long already, but you never dared to. From something like that you could be freed in one day?

Yet it is possible! And what's more: it happens very often that people are totally free of their dependence on smoking in one day. Actually, it's not even one day that is needed, but just one moment: the moment that you decide that you don't have to smoke anymore. Very few people experience such a moment spontaneously, this sudden feeling of "I've had it, I don't need this anymore," and stop smoking for the rest of their lives.

Most smokers think almost daily about quitting, but hold back for fear of their lives becoming terribly difficult without cigarettes. What the Free Yourself Method does for you is to deprogram all of the thoughts and feelings that chain you to smoking, so that you will have a free choice again. You tell me, if you didn't feel the compulsion, if smoking didn't even taste good anymore, and if you really felt free to choose to be a smoker for the rest of your life or a non-smoker, wouldn't you choose to quit?

But wait a minute: deprogramming? Isn't that something like brainwashing? No, but you could call it the undoing of being brainwashed. It's the smoker who suffers from a typical kind of brainwashing, the kind that we call "psychological addiction." It's the smoker who thinks that she needs to breathe in smoke before she can become sociable. It's the smoker who is afraid to stop doing something that very slowly destroys him. It's the smoker that spends a fortune on something that she is sometimes ashamed of, something that makes her feel guilty, and something that she would like to quit doing. It's the smoker who knows all these things for a long time already, but feels too weak to quit. It's the smoker who is brainwashed, and the Free Yourself Method breaks the delusion. After that, you are free to walk through life as a non-smoker.

You can also look at it this way: Every smoker has a certain image, a certain way of thinking and feeling about his addiction. This way of looking makes him dependent on smoking. There is also another way of looking at smoking—the way of the non-smoker. As soon as you switch to the non-smoker's outlook, you're freed from smoking. Such a switch is called a "Gestaltswitch" in psychology.

Figure 1

Figure 1 shows an old woman or a young girl, depending on the image that you see the first time you look at it. Do you only see one of the possibilities? Keep looking. The big hook nose of the old woman is at the same time the left cheek of the young girl. The mouth of the old woman is the collar of the young woman. The left eye of the old woman is the left ear of the young one. Do you see it? If you still only see one of the possibilities, just keep reading and look once in a while at the picture.

Show it to somebody else if you want to, until you see both possibilities. The switching from one possibility to the other always happens in one moment. For some people this can be a true revelation. While reading this book this could happen to you: that you suddenly get another outlook on smoking. This can be accompanied by emotions, and when you experience this, you are actually already freed from smoking. But also in that case you can still keep smoking until you have finished reading this book.

Still, this transition from smoker to non-smoker doesn't have to be so abrupt. It can also be a more gradual process. At the end of the book you have a totally different outlook on smoking than you had at the start, without being able to tell when your "smoker's outlook" changed into a "non-smoker's outlook." Figure 2 gives an example of this.

Figure 2: changing images, man's head—woman's body.

At the end of the series, you see a different image from the one seen at the start, but you can't really tell where the change occurs. Whether the change from smoker to non-smoker occurs abruptly or gradually, the result will be the same: You will no longer feel forced to light a cigarette. You are free to take the step towards a life without addiction.

But first, you'll have to concern yourself with the question what this addiction is exactly. I'm talking about free choice all the time, and that means that we also have to take a look at the alternative: to keep smoking. Let's investigate in an open and unbiased way the possibility of continuing to smoke. The question is: Is there a way to become a happy smoker?

Chapter 4

The Happy Smoker Doesn't Exist

Why would you quit smoking? It's sociable. It tastes good. It's cheaper than all other drugs, and it helps you in difficult situations. So why do you have to be freed from it? True you may get cancer later, but that chance is only one in four! And maybe you'll be run over by a cab before that time. Then you would have quit smoking for nothing!

For twenty-five years, I kept looking for ways of being happy with smoking. I denied all the bad sides of smoking. Dying sooner? I told myself that it was a nice thing not to become so old. I wanted to live a great and exciting life, and I wanted to die in the saddle. Less energy? But I don't need more energy. I'm not a sports type and for the things I like to do, I already have enough energy. Unhealthy? Well, those few rasping, coughing fits every day... I just have a little cold all the time, that's all. Does it stink? Doesn't bother me, I have a permanent stuffy nose, so I don't smell it. Loss of taste and smell? I can still taste the difference between ketchup and mayonnaise. And to smell less in this polluted society is an advantage.

In this way, I turned the disadvantages into advantages. But in the back of my head was always this little voice, whispering very softly, "That's a bunch of bull."

"If only I could smoke just a few cigarettes a day, I would never quit," I thought for a long time. Just like every heavy smoker, I was jealous of the "social smokers." Those people seem to us the personification of the happy smoker. Once I quit smoking for two years. I started smoking again, because I thought: "Now I've proven that I'm in control of my smoking, so now I can smoke one from time to time." Forget it. The first months I smoked a lot less than one pack a day, but I missed every cigarette that I didn't smoke. And gradually the lines that I had drawn around smoking disappeared.

Now I have discovered that the happy smoker doesn't exist. There are two important misconceptions about the happy (since moderate) smoker. The first one is that the heavy smoker can evolve into a moderate smoker. I was a heavy smoker, and all my attempts to smoke less ended in smoking more. And if I'm honest, I seldom really tried to smoke less; I very often planned it though.

Are you a heavy smoker? If smoking less would be a way of smoking happily, wouldn't you have already done it? Be honest with yourself, and admit that you're just not the type to smoke a little.

The second misconception about the happy smoker is the idea that a moderate smoker is not addicted (or that he is less addicted). A woman came to see me who smoked three or four cigarettes a day; she always started after dinner. She wanted to quit smoking very badly. Although she looked forward to smoking those cigarettes after dinner, she also dreaded them more and more.

Why? Because, she disliked the taste of those cigarettes, and yet she couldn't keep herself from lighting them. She was addicted.

For the heavy smoker, this is an incredible story. Who wants to quit smoking when you only smoke a few cigarettes a day? Every heavy smoker is jealous of the moderate smoker. Compare this with the prisoner who is locked in a small cell and is never allowed outside. This prisoner is jealous of the prisoner who is allowed to walk in the courtyard an hour a day. But nobody holds you in your smoke addiction, except you! Why be jealous of someone in the same prison? Wouldn't it be better to choose total freedom?

Of course, someone feels "less unhealthy" when she smokes two cigarettes instead of twenty. But is the unhealthy feeling the most important reason to want to quit smoking? The lady who smoked a few cigarettes a day knew better. She didn't feel unhealthy; she felt imprisoned, and that's why she wanted be free from smoking. How many times in my smoking life have I thought, "I wish I would only have to smoke those cigarettes that really tasted good and could leave the other ones out." This highlights the most distinguishing feature of addiction—that you are not free anymore in your choice of using or not using. It's this lack of freedom, this realization that you are doing something that you don't agree with that provokes feeling unhappy.

When my youngest daughter brought home a drawing of her coughing father on his deathbed, I didn't feel my own fear of death. No, I felt her fear of losing me, and because I love her with all my heart, I wanted to take away every fear that she had. In this case, I could only produce a guilty smile. And I did feel deeply unhappy for a moment. Then I repressed that feeling as quickly as possible and felt the urgent need for a cigarette (that I smoked out of sight of my daughter, of course). That's how a smoker often has to lick the wounds that he inflicts upon himself. And sometimes he thinks: How long does this have to go on?

There is another reason why smokers believe that happy smokers exist. They remember themselves having a lot less trouble with smoking when they were younger. Every smoker longs for the starting period of his smoking, because then he was young and fit, but mainly because he didn't realize that he was addicted yet. The idea that once upon a time, you smoked without it bothering you at all keeps the illusion alive that it's possible to experience this again. That's one of the delusions of the addict. But a distinguishing feature of addiction is that you sink into it deeper and deeper, that it bothers you more and more, and that you want to get rid of it more and more. Once you are addicted, you can never become less addicted, only more. For the addict, the past seems always better than the future. That's because addiction is a process of decay: Every day, every month, every year you lose a part of your health and your vitality. Nobody can be really happy with that idea.

The happy smoker doesn't exist, because every smoker (who actually inhales the smoke) is addicted. The fact that some smokers smoke more than others has different causes. It could be that one smoker dislikes the taste of cigarettes more than the other. Or that one smoker just likes to deny himself a few cigarettes a day. Or that the other smoker has developed a pattern in which she never starts smoking before three o'clock. Every smoker notices at some point that he can't refrain from it anymore. Usually, this realization comes after a few months of smoking regularly. Some people will find this idea so unacceptable that they build in certain periods of non-smoking, just to prove that they are not addicted. Somebody like that will say with a lot of conviction: "I only smoke when I really want to." When you have finished this book, you will see that this sentence sounds just as silly as the man who hits his big toe a few times with a hammer and then says, "I only do this when I really want to."

If you're still in doubt, if you think that for you there might be a possibility to change from an addicted smoker into a happy one, then stop reading now and make the decision to start smoking in that way. Start right away! Why wait? And only go on reading when you have failed in your attempt.

But when you realize that there is no way to become a happy smoker, that at the very most you can only temporarily repress your displeasure and close your eyes to your addiction while in the background you will always have these ambiguous feelings, that you will always go back and forth between the fear of missing smoking and the longing to get rid of it—always this double-hearted feeling of yearning for and being disgusted by smoking—when you realize that you want to be free of this oppressive situation, then read on.

Are you afraid to read on? Then read on, by all means. Don't you also want to be free of that fear? The actual quitting of cigarette smoking is the last step in quitting smoking. First one has to end the ambiguous feelings, the negativity, the psychological dependence. After that, quitting is a breeze.

Chapter 5

What Does a Cigarette Do For You?

Example 1: You are at home behind your desk. In front of you is the letter from the company where you recently applied for a job. In the letter you are being asked to call the company about an appointment for a follow up interview. You are thinking about what you're going to say. You light a cigarette. The cigarette helps you fight the stress. At least, that's what you think.

Example 2: You are coming out of a busy meeting, in which some stressful subjects were being discussed. You are at home and fragments of the conversation go through your head. You feel tense and light a cigarette. That will help you to relax. At least, that's what you think.

Example 3: You have a two-hour layover in the airport and you are bored. You finished the newspaper and decide to go outside to the curb to smoke a cigarette. That will help fight the boredom. At least that's what you think.

Example 4: At home you are working on a difficult project. It's an interesting assignment with a lot of challenges, and you will have to stay focussed on different things at the same time. You're working on smart solutions and are losing yourself in the work. You smoke a lot during this project. By smoking you can concentrate harder. At least, that's what you think.

Below you can find a schematic representation of human activities, in which the division passive-active is distinguished from the division positive-negative. The four examples above, and a lot of other examples with smoking as an important component, can be placed in this model. Waiting and insecurity are usually felt as negative and passive experiences. Anger and stress are also experienced as negative, but they have to do with activity. With positive experiences, it's possible to make the division active-passive as well. Relaxing, a nice conversation, and watching TV are passive experiences. Creative works like writing, painting, or concentrating on a puzzle are active experiences.

Something strange is going on here: Smoking appears to be a device that's being used in situations that are diametrical opposites. How can something that works against stress also work against boredom? How can something that helps one to concentrate also help one to relax?

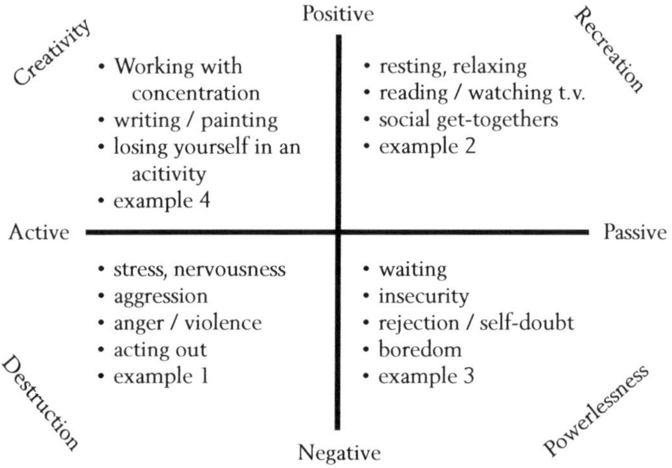

Figure 3: Smoking helps in diametrically opposed situations.

I will show you how weird this actually is by using another example. Suppose you would go to the doctor and say, "Doctor, I'm having a hard time relaxing lately, do you have something for me?" The doctor gives you pills that appear to work really well. Every time you feel tense, you take one of these pills, and after some time you feel a lot calmer. After a few months, you go to the doctor again, because you have to take an exam and you have some trouble concentrating. The doctor says, "Yes, I have a fine medicine for that. You should take the same pills that I gave you to relax the other day. They will help you to concentrate as well. This is really a fantastic medicine, because it also works against boredom, it gives you more self esteem, helps against depression and makes you feel better after a meal. It helps you to wake up in the morning and it also helps you to sleep better at night. Here is the whole bag! Have fun."

Honestly, you wouldn't fall for it if it were pills, would you? One simply can't use the same pill for totally different problems. Although there is one exception. In the medical world there are these pills that are called placebos. They only contain chalk and have a colored sugar coating, so by themselves their effectiveness is zero, zip, nothing. Still, they seem to work in a lot of cases.

A lot of scientific research concerns the way this placebo effect works. One of the results is that the more the patient trusts his doctor, the higher the effectiveness of the pill. Of course, the patient is not aware that it is a fake medication. Another research result: the brighter the color of the pill, the higher the effectiveness.

The effectiveness of a placebo pill is one hundred percent dependent on the belief of the user in the effectiveness. Although the use of placebos is not without debate, one could also see them as proof for the power of the human mind. When a fake pill really works, just because one believes that it works, then, in fact, it's the mind—after taking the detour of trusting the doctor and the medicine—that heals.

So the same medicine can only work against different diseases when it is a placebo medicine, when the medicine itself has no effectiveness whatsoever. This is also true of smoking. Smoking helps against boredom, but also against stress. It helps one concentrate and it helps one to relax. That can only be true if smoking doesn't have any effectiveness by itself!

Compare it with all other addictive substances that our society is rich in! There are uplifting ones that you take when you want to have more energy, and calming and relaxing ones when you want to take it easy. In the world of drugs, the names are "uppers" and "downers." Don't give a raver opium before he goes to a party, because there won't be much of a party for him. With opium, he'd rather stay home, stare out of a window and listen to quiet Indian music.

All drugs have a specific effect upon the user. Even with the lightly uplifting drug caffeine, the effect is unambiguous and unmistakable. You drink coffee to wake up in the morning, but you don't drink it to become sleepy at night as well. With nicotine, this is different. Because nicotine doesn't have an effect of its own. That's why you can use nicotine in every situation. That's why you can combine smoking with all other drugs. And that usually happens, because practically every drug addict is also addicted to smoking.

So smoking doesn't have its own effect and is dependent on the belief of the user. "But I'm not crazy," you might think now. "Smoking does help me in a lot of situations!" Don't worry, I'm not saying that you are crazy, I'm only saying that you are addicted. That's why you have a certain image of reality: the image of an addict. Don't forget that I myself smoked for twenty-five years, and all that time I was convinced of the effect of nicotine. Now I have another outlook on smoking—the outlook of a non-smoker. But I didn't forget the old outlook of the addicted smoker. The outlook and the feeling of the non-smoker are a lot more pleasant to have than the outlook and feeling of a smoker. I'm trying to show you the outlook of the non-smoker in this book. Because once you see that, you'll get rid of smoking for good.

Now, your common sense tells you: Smoking doesn't do anything; it doesn't have any effect of it's own. Your feelings, however, tell you: Smoking helps me in various situations. How is that possible? You are not crazy, are you? The only possible explanation for this opposition between common sense and your feelings is the fact that you are addicted. It's the addiction that makes you believe in the effect of nicotine, that makes you feel that smoking helps you in a lot of situations, that makes you enjoy smoking. But how is that possible? How can addiction be such a big influence on the way one looks at the world and on the way one feels? Lo and behold: Read the next chapter.

Chapter 6

Contradictory Physical Reactions to Nicotine

Nicotine is a substance without color and without scent that can be found in tobacco in small quantities. It is very quickly absorbed into the blood—within a few seconds after the inhaling of cigarette smoke. Nicotine is poisonous and was used in earlier days as poison in produce, to fight lice and other pests. The body reacts to this poison with a defense mechanism, by narrowing the blood vessels and by eliminating it as soon as possible. After half an hour, half of the nicotine has disappeared from the blood; after another half-hour, half of the other half, and so on. After a few days of not smoking every trace of nicotine will have left your body.

Nicotine is not only poisonous; it's also addictive. That means that the body protests against the disappearance of nicotine from the body. This protesting is done by physical withdrawal. This is a light feeling of emptiness, a hollow feeling. It can best be compared to feeling a little bit hungry. These signs of physical withdrawal are so light that most smokers don't even realize they feel it many times a day. Every time one doesn't smoke a cigarette for longer then half an hour, these physical withdrawal signs will start. It's only the mind that sometimes makes out of these hardly noticeable signs an enormous feeling of withdrawal. Imagine the next situation:

You are driving your car and you are in a great mood. Just before, you have had a break to eat at a restaurant. You've had some nice food, a cigarette with the coffee, and on you go for the last two hours of the trip. It was half an hour ago that you extinguished your last cigarette. You feel great; you don't need a cigarette yet. You only have a passing thought about with what exit you will smoke your next cigarette. Everything under control! Suddenly, you realize with a shock that your cigarettes are not on the dashboard where they always are. Quickly you feel in your coat pocket. Gone! You have forgotten your cigarettes on the table in the restaurant! You feel slightly panicky. Suddenly, you feel the strong urge to smoke and in a bad mood you calculate how far it is to the next gas station.

Also, when you get up in the morning your body hasn't had any nicotine for a whole night, so there are physical withdrawal symptoms. Still there are a lot of smokers who don't want to smoke at all before their breakfast or first cup of coffee. The mind is used to certain events or a certain time at which to start smoking and before that time the physical withdrawal is simply ignored. These signs of physical withdrawal are there the whole day, each time that you haven't smoked a cigarette for longer than half an hour. But the feeling of needing a cigarette is purely psychological and can suddenly occur, depending on a situation or event. Even if the second before there was not a thought of smoking at all. That's what the psychological addiction does: It makes a mountain (yearning for a cigarette) out of a molehill (very light physical withdrawal).

So nicotine has a double effect on the body. On the one hand, the body reacts defensively: the vessels narrow, the poison is eliminated as soon as possible, the lungs protest by producing extra phlegm to get the tar residue out of there, the throat sometimes protests against irritation by a coughing fit.

At the same time, the body resists the elimination of nicotine from the blood. This physical withdrawal is sometimes noticeable as a lightly hollow feeling in the stomach.

So the body resists the taking in of nicotine as well as the departure of the nicotine. This physical inconsistency forms the basis for the psychological inconsistency that every smoker experiences: The longing to be freed from this filthy and unhealthy habit opposed to the fear for withdrawal, the panic that you can feel when you think of a life without cigarettes. Because, as in the example, it's already so hard to get to the next gas station without cigarettes. How hard it must be then not to be able to smoke the rest of your life! Here we have the basis of the fear that every smoker feels when he thinks of quitting. It's the typical fear of the addicted. Before the end of this book you will read how to get rid of this fear in one day. It is so ridiculously simple that I will need a lot of chapters to prepare you for it. Otherwise, you wouldn't believe your own eyes and your own feeling.

First, we will go into the psychological aspects of smoking. Why does it feel as if smoking has an effect on you, while we have just concluded on logical grounds that this can not be the case? Prepare yourself for some shocking insights!

Chapter 7

The Effect of Nicotine

What does nicotine actually do? The answer to this question is as simple as it is astounding: Nicotine causes withdrawal. And it does this between about fifteen and thirty minutes after the smoking of a cigarette. Physically, these withdrawal symptoms don't amount to much. The human mind interprets these symptoms however as a void, as a need that can only be fulfilled by another cigarette. During and right after the smoking of a cigarette, one doesn't experience withdrawal. So it seems that the smoking of the cigarette ends the withdrawal. In reality, however, the cigarette causes the withdrawal, while the withdrawal of the previous cigarette is temporarily relieved. It's only during and right after smoking a cigarette that you don't feel the need for a cigarette. In fact, that's the only moment that you feel like a non-smoker because you aren't feeling withdrawal pangs. How strange that the only reason to keep lighting cigarettes is to get back the feelings you had as a non-smoker, free of compulsions and yearnings for a cigarette.

So the yearning for a cigarette is nothing more than the longing to be freed from the burden of withdrawal, to be freed from the dependent feeling, to be freed from thoughts about smoking. Every cigarette actually gives us the illusion of freedom, the illusion of not being addicted, the illusion that we smoke by choice because we like it, instead of out of a compulsion that forces us to do something that we don't agree with. But so frail is this illusion, so quickly it disappears, and we find ourselves again confined by our dependence. To realize how pathetic this vicious circle is, consider the following comparison.

Assume that you are in a cell, the symbolic jail of the smoke addiction. The longer you postpone the smoking of a cigarette, the clearer your neurotic thoughts become about needing a cigarette. In our comparison this means: The better you see the bars of your jail. This confinement gets less and less bearable. You just have to light a cigarette to be freed for a while from your compulsion. It is as if the prisoner pulls a black bag over his head in order not to see the bars of his smoke jail. But the more you smoke, the more suffocating this bag becomes. After the extinguishing of the cigarette, the bag comes off your head and you get fresh air again. But the bars of your cell are still there, and it doesn't take long before they start to disturb you again. Until you can't take it anymore and light another cigarette: Again this choking mask in order not to see those bars for a while. Thus, the prisoner fools himself dozens of times a day with the illusion that he's not imprisoned. But read closely, because the most bizarre aspect of this comparison is yet to come: Why are you in this prison anyway? It is the punishment for putting that black bag over your head! The moment you decide never to pull that black bag over your head anymore, the door of the prison will open and you will be free from any compulsive thought about smoking. The moment you decide to end this disturbing addiction, hardly any withdrawal symptom will appear anymore, no more compulsive thinking. Then you will be free and you will never have to suffocate yourself anymore.

Here is another example. You are at your desk, concentrating on your work. It's summertime and the window is open, but the sounds from outside hardly reach you. You are totally absorbed by your work and you didn't notice yet that your neighbor started mowing his lawn with a noisy machine. Slowly, some irritation about this noise starts growing in the back of your head. Suddenly it is too much: you jump up and shut the window. Because of the storm window, hardly any noise comes through now. What a relief! What a pleasant, free feeling! After a while this pleasant feeling fades away. Would you open the window to let the noise in again, in order to enjoy the silence after you have closed it again? Because that is the enjoyment of a cigarette: the elimination of an irritation that it caused in the first place!

Another comparison. It's a well-known fact that a mosquito bite or poison ivy can cause a lot of itching. When you don't touch the itchy spot, the itch disappears sooner than when you start scratching. Even so, we usually scratch, because that is such a good feeling, and the itch is so irritating. Also with scratching, the itching fortunately goes away after a while. Fortunately? But that scratching felt so good! Then why aren't we disappointed when the itching goes away? That's because the scratching only feels good, because it makes the itching go away for some time. But when the itching is gone, we are very happy about that. We won't go looking for some fresh poison ivy in a forest in order to enjoy scratching the itch. Because that is the enjoyment of a cigarette: to scratch in order not to feel the itch that is caused by the scratching!

Let's take a closer look at this example. So you accidentally ran into this poison ivy. For a long time, you are scratching already. At the start, this scratching felt good, but now it is starting to bother you. What if you knew for sure that the itching never, and I mean never would go away if you kept scratching? What if you knew that the itching would grow worse because of the scratching?

What if you knew that the scratching could give you a lot of other problems? And what if somebody would tell you that the itching would go away very quickly if you would stop scratching? Wouldn't you stop scratching immediately? Why is quitting smoking so hard exactly? BUT IT IS NOT!

Quitting smoking is ridiculously easy. It's only the fear of quitting that makes it hard to make a decision. And what is it that we are afraid of? We are afraid of failing in our attempt and of being confronted even more with our weakness and with being a prisoner of smoking. And we are also afraid of succeeding in our attempt, so that we will miss the smoking for the rest of our lives. Both fears—the failure of quitting and the success of it—belong to the addiction. Both fears will disappear the moment you quit in the right way. Later in this book, I will come back to these fears. First, it is important to look a little closer at the effects of nicotine, so that it will become clearer to you what the physical aspect of your smoke addiction is, and what comprises the mental.

Chapter 8

Graphic Representation of the Effect of Nicotine

To clarify the exact effect of nicotine in different situations, I have been looking for a way to represent the effect of nicotine in graphically. At first, I tried simple little graphs that compared the smoking of a cigarette with not smoking in the same situation. What happens when you light a cigarette in a stressful situation and what happens if you don't? The graphs showed some nice peaks and valleys, but didn't give any new information. By comparing the smoking of a cigarette in a certain situation with the not smoking of it, I confined myself to the outlook of an addicted smoker. Turning it around, I decided to compare the effects of smoking in a certain situation with the same situation as experienced by a non-smoker. The graphs are now more revealing.

In the next chapters you will find some graphs, for situations involving stress, concentration, relaxation, and boredom. Right below is a general representation of the effect of nicotine. The vertical axis measures the subjective well-being of the smoker. Positive (up) means that you feel better, negative (down) means that you feel worse. Of course, thousands of other factors in life determine whether you feel good or bad. These are all left out of the graph for convenience's sake. This means that the horizontal dotted line shows a neutral level of well being. You can also say that the horizontal dotted line shows the level of well being of a non-smoker. The continuous line shows the well being of a smoker, related to the non-smoker in the same situation.

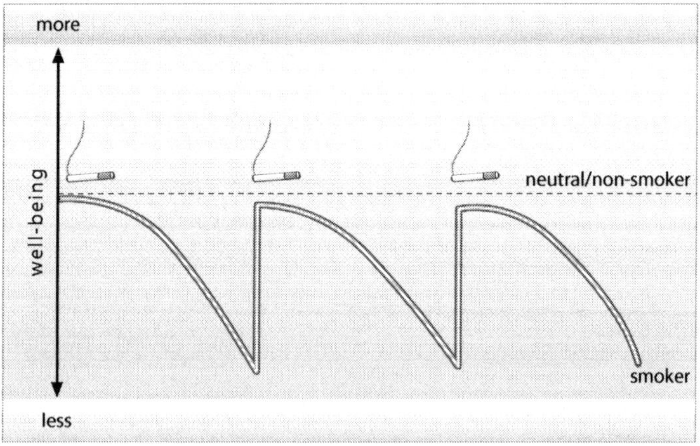

Graph 1: The general effect of nicotine.

A graph has to start somewhere. The actual beginning would be the very first cigarette. But then we would get a very long graph. The graph below starts in the very near past, about four or five cigarettes ago, exactly at the moment of the lighting of that cigarette. During the smoking of this cigarette, the smoker doesn't experience any withdrawal, no compulsive thoughts of smoking: in short, his well being is the same as that of a non-smoker. After the extinguishing of that cigarette, the body starts immediately to eliminate the nicotine. Pretty soon, some light withdrawal symptoms arise. The smoker will hardly notice them in the beginning. After a while though, these withdrawal symptoms bring about the idea of lighting another cigarette. This idea becomes stronger and stronger, and your feeling of well being will dive faster and faster. Then you light another cigarette. Within seconds your discomfort disappears, the withdrawal symptoms disappear, the compulsive thoughts disappear, and you experience for a moment the illusion of liberation. Your level of well being comes close to that of the non-smoker. It only comes close? Yes, after a while a certain amount of habituation results from the effect of nicotine, so that you will always maintain a certain amount of discomfort, even while you're smoking. If every cigarette is an attempt to feel like a non-smoker, the success of this attempt becomes more and more remote. So every cigarette eliminates the withdrawal symptoms of the previous one only partly. Besides, you experience more and more troublesome side effects: the cigarette doesn't taste so good anymore; the coughing fits spoil your enjoyment; and you feel dependent, unhealthy, and weak.

This shows the tragedy of any addiction: Begun with the intention to feel better than before, you sink deeper and deeper in the spiral of idle attempts to feel less bad than before. Idle attempts to compensate your withdrawal symptoms with a new dose. Idle attempts to feel like someone who is not addicted for a while. All the while, every attempt only makes you sink deeper in the swamp of addiction. What a blissful thought that you can escape very soon! It is so easy—you only have to keep on reading.

Chapter 9

Smoking In Negative Active Situations

In Chapter Five, we saw a schematic representation of the different situations in which we use smoking to help us, to support us. Smoking helps with positive as well as negative feelings, in passive as well as active situations. In the next chapters, I will explore this further. Every smoker thinks that a cigarette helps him in tense, negative situations, such as stress. We already saw that, logically speaking, a cigarette can't possibly have any effect, and that the effect of nicotine can be compared to the so-called placebo effect—where medication doesn't have any physical effect but helps with illness, due to the belief of the user. Thus, you feel that a cigarette really helps fight the stress. The fact that your feeling deviates from your common sense shows that you are addicted. The addiction makes it appear as if the cigarette has a soothing effect. In reality, smoking doesn't fight stress at all; it creates it!

Picture the following situation: You are at home at your desk. In a few moments, you are going to make a phone call that is extremely important to you. It could be a conversation with your boss about an upcoming resignation, or with your ex-lover about coming back together again. A non-smoker also feels the tension rising before she picks up the phone, and also during the conversation she feels a lot of stress. Only when the phone is put down does the tension release.

In Graph 2, this situation is represented. I assume that the smoker has just smoked a cigarette at the start

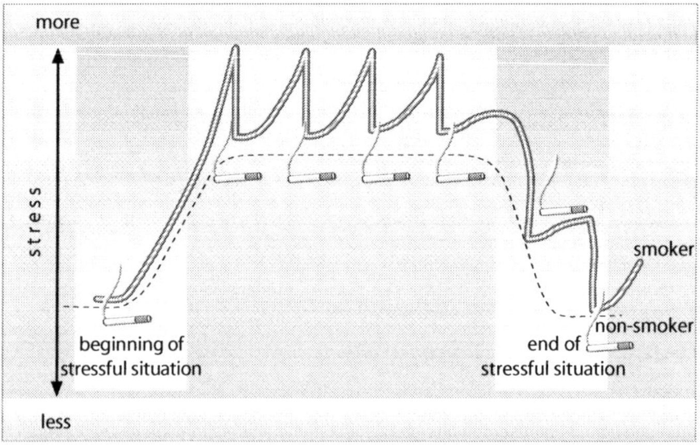

Graph 2: Smoking induces stress.

of this graph, so he doesn't suffer any withdrawal. The vertical axis in the graph represents the amount of stress: up means more stress, down means less. The dotted line shows the course of the stress for a non-smoker. At the start, the stress level for the smoker and the non-smoker is the same. But while the tension is rising, besides the stress that is inherent in the situation, the smoker experiences another kind of stress as well: the increasing withdrawal. These two kinds of stress are inseparable for the smoker; they feel like one kind of stress, so his stress increases more quickly than the stress of the non-smoker. The smoker feels extra tense and lights a cigarette. What happens to the stress level now? Right: it goes down a little bit, because the withdrawal stress is temporarily eliminated. The stress inherent in the situation stays the same, of course. So smoking only helps to fight the part of the stress caused by withdrawal symptoms of smoking. In short, smoking only helps to fight the stress that is caused by smoking.

It is not only the case that smoking doesn't help to fight stress. Reality is even more tragic, because smoking induces stress. How can that be? Well, I already stated that each cigarette only succeeds partially in eliminating the withdrawal caused by the previous one, because of a gradually growing immunity. But there are more important reasons why smoking induces stress. I will clarify this with an example.

In at least ten of the twenty-five years that I smoked, I rolled my own cigarettes. In the situation of an important telephone conversation as described above, I had to role some extras in case the talk took a long time. Every smoker's worry, to be suddenly out of cigarettes, or not to be able to reach them, is an extra stress factor. And what to think of the stressful situation in which you are not even allowed to smoke? (Like a job interview.) The result is extra stress. In fact, this feeling of dependence, the worry never to be without your "ciggy," is a permanent stress factor. Thus, the smoker always suffers from a higher stress level than the non-smoker in the same situation.

Are you scared to have to go into all these difficult situations without smoking after you quit? Very understandable. I was also scared and insecure when I thought of quitting smoking. That's what addiction does to you: It makes you afraid and insecure. Now that I don't smoke anymore, I deal with difficult situations with a lot more self-confidence. As it happens, I found a much better means for dealing with stress.

It's very simple. Stress happens to be a very human phenomenon. Everybody feels stress in certain situations. When I find myself in a situation that makes me feel tense, I tell myself, "There you have more proof that you're a human being." I also don't try to hide my anxiety. Stress drops immediately after you have accepted it as something normal. The residue of tension is often simply necessary to function a little better.

In short, life doesn't become harder when you don't smoke anymore. On the contrary, the stress even decreases, because you are no longer dependent on breathing in smoke to be able to deal with difficulties. Smoking doesn't solve any problem. Quitting smoking solves one problem: the smoking problem. You've figured that much out now: smoking is a problem, not a solution to a problem. Smoking is stress, not a means to combat stress.

Chapter 10

Smoking In Positive Active Situations

One of the most persistent misconceptions about smoking is the idea that it helps in positive active situations such as with creative work and jobs that require a high level of concentration. When I still smoked, I worked for a couple of years in computer automation. The more I had to concentrate, the more I smoked. Sometimes I had three burning cigarettes in my ashtray next to the keyboard. That's how automatically I lit them. Masses of programmers and IT-specialists smoke like chimneys while they're watching the screen and thinking up complicated procedures. But this cliché image also prevails about writers—that they can only start working when

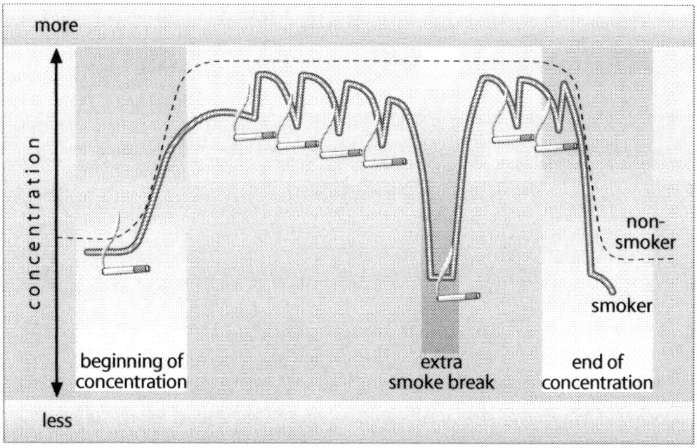

Graph 3: Smoking decreases the ability to concentrate.

the bottle of whiskey and the package of cigarettes are at hand, next to an old Underwood manual typewriter. All these people are wrong. Not because they are crazy, by the way, but because they are addicted. Smoking doesn't increase concentration at all. On the contrary, it decreases the ability to concentrate.

In Graph 3, the vertical axis shows the level of concentration during a certain work situation. The higher the line, the higher and more intense the level of concentration. In this graph, the course of concentration of the smoker is also compared to that of a non-smoker in a similar situation. This situation starts with a relaxed condition, after which an exciting and complicated job is being done, and ends again with relaxation. The dotted line shows the course of concentration of a non-smoker. I assume that the smoker has just smoked a cigarette at the start of the difficult job. At the start, his concentration level will rise about as fast as that of the non-smoker. Within several minutes, both will be at the top of their concentration ability. It won't take long, however, before the smoker begins to experience withdrawal symptoms.

Everybody knows how it goes with concentration. A small distraction can totally disrupt it. Is your youngest son screaming in the bathroom that you have to pull up his pants? Is your neighbor testing his new motorized hedge shears? Do they suddenly play that irritating song on the radio? At first, you don't hear a thing because you are so concentrated on the job. A few seconds later, you've totally lost your groove. Because that's how it goes with concentration: you are totally in it or totally out of it.

As soon as you experience the first symptoms of withdrawal, and a small loss of concentration because of that, you light a new cigarette. For you know from experience that if you don't do that, you will totally lose your concentration on very short notice. After the lighting of that cigarette, your concentration comes back to the same level, albeit not all the way. After all, the withdrawal from the previous cigarette is not totally undone by the smoking of the next.

Thus, a smoker has to keep smoking constantly to prevent his concentration from diminishing. Yet, a smoker never reaches the level of concentration of a non-smoker. Because while you're concentrating, you have to light a cigarette from time-to-time, sometimes you have to take the cigarette up or put it down again, so there are short moments of lost concentration all the time. Besides, a smoker will need a cup of coffee or tea a lot more often, to get rid of that filthy taste in his throat. That's why smokers usually take a lot more short breaks while working.

What smoking actually does, instead of enhancing the concentration, is prevent a loss of concentration. A person that is addicted to smoking can't concentrate without smoking. Still, the smoking causes a loss of concentration for several reasons. The smoker is a little distracted every time by the mild withdrawal symptoms and by the lighting of a cigarette to fight these symptoms. In this fight, he only partially succeeds. Moreover, less oxygen is supplied to the smoker's brain, because of his badly functioning lungs and his overall worse condition. For these reasons, his ability to concentrate is ten per cent less. All in all, smoking makes for a significant decrease in the ability to concentrate.

It's actually a tragic image, how you're sitting there as a smoker, smoking your head off to keep concentrating, while the result will always be a lot less than your natural ability. Do you have work that you need to concentrate hard for? Are you scared to have to do that work without smoking? That's understandable. For that is what smoking does to you: It makes you dependent and scared. Dependent on cigarettes and scared to have to do without them. Wouldn't you rather get rid of that fear? Wouldn't you rather be free and independent and trust your own capacities instead of an addictive device?

Since I don't smoke anymore, I can concentrate a lot better. That happened right away, from the first days after quitting. I also work longer at a time now. As a smoker, I took smoking breaks every fifteen or thirty minutes. Now I can sometimes be so absorbed in my work, suddenly looking up, checking my watch, only to discover that I have been working non-stop for two hours in a row. That is such a good feeling, to be able to concentrate one hundred per cent, without being constantly distracted by the urge to light a cigarette. I wholeheartedly recommend it.

Chapter 11

Smoking In Negative Passive Situations

Negative passive situations are situations in which you are uncomfortable, insecure, forced to be inactive, or not able to break your passivity. A lot of these situations are characterized by boredom. Boredom can be a period of forced inactivity while you feel like doing something. An example is a long, boring plane flight. Boredom can also involve a period of forced activity, when you feel like doing nothing, or you feel like doing something else. A security guard standing at the entrance of a shop the whole day, who is bored to death, comes to mind. Boredom is a condition that you don't choose, but that happens to you. Sometimes it arises out of circumstances, sometimes from within, because you feel blocked. Boredom is a condition in which you can never feel happy. Or, the other way around: when you feel happy doing nothing, you don't call that boredom, but you call it being lazy or resting or meditation or the like. Boredom is an involuntary condition of powerlessness.

Do you see the resemblance with being addicted? Being addicted is also a condition of powerlessness, of not being free to choose. Nobody ever chooses to become addicted. It just happens to you. While you are bored, you often feel bad about yourself. You feel too weak to break the impasse. As an addict, you also feel weak, not able to break the addiction. The saying goes "I'm bored to death." Addiction kills you in the long run. Both are manifestations of self-destruction.

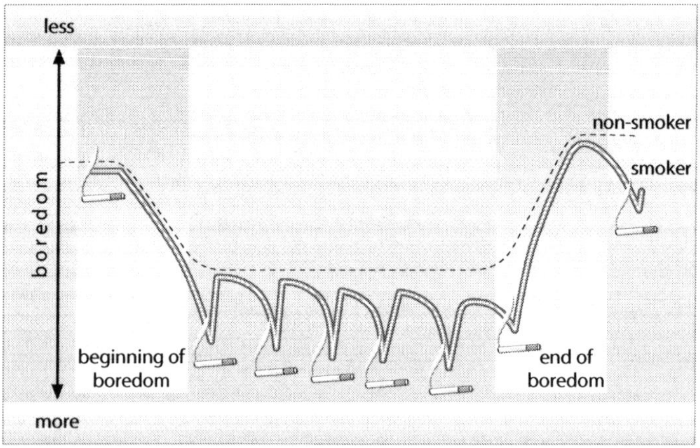

Graph 4: Smoking doesn't help to fight boredom.

During a period of boredom, a smoker smokes more and more. The smoking appears to fight the boredom. But that's an illusion. Look at Graph 4. A non-smoker is obviously also bored from time-to-time. Her wellbeing diminishes when she gets bored. In the graph, the increase of boredom is shown as a descent of the line. After a while, the boredom goes away, because the circumstances change (e.g. the plane arrives), or because you decided to do something yourself.

The smoker is bored like the non-smoker. But for the smoker, another uncomfortable factor arises, namely the withdrawal from the previous cigarette. This withdrawal is only a very slight feeling of discomfort that easily mixes with other feelings of discomfort. Like the boredom. After a while, the discomfort becomes too strong and the smoker lights a cigarette. Immediately the feeling of discomfort lessens, because he has mainly eliminated the withdrawal. It's seems as if he is suddenly a little less bored. Still, the feeling of discomfort isn't any less than that of the non-smoker in the same situation. As a smoker, one feels almost constantly worse than a non-smoker, except during the smoking of a cigarette.

So the smoker knows that he can lessen his feeling of discomfort during a period of boredom by lighting a cigarette. In fact, he only lessens the withdrawal of the previous cigarette. When you're bored and really have nothing else to do, very soon after you have extinguished your cigarette, you want the bad feeling to go away again. Actually, you would have to wait until you have built up enough withdrawal symptoms, so at least for a half-hour. But because you're bored, you smoke more and more. A reverse effect arises. The smoking hardly eliminates withdrawal, because that didn't have time to kick in yet. But because of all the smoking you start to feel "smoked" yourself and every cigarette tastes worse than the previous one. You feel so powerless against this compulsive smoking and you curse your boredom that makes you smoke so compulsively. Your feeling of well being goes down the longer the boredom lasts. The non-smoker only feels bad because of his boredom. But you as a smoker feel twice as bad, because of the boredom and because of the compulsive smoking.

Of course, as a smoker you can at least enjoy the activity of lighting a cigarette. It seems as if you have something to do for a moment. This action is not the result of a free choice though, but of the compulsive thought that smoking helps to fight boredom. A compulsive thought like that doesn't fight the boredom; you do it out of boredom. Besides, it keeps you from finding creative solutions to fight the boredom. A non-smoker is generally better capable of fighting boredom. Here is an example from my own past.

My parents live in France, and once in a while I get in my car to drive there. It's a ten to twelve-hour drive, mainly on the expressway. During these long, boring trips I used to smoke like crazy. Halfway through the trip,

I already felt totally "smoked out." For the duration of the rest of the trip, I would be in a constant battle with myself to postpone the next cigarette as long as possible. Of course, I did that with the help of a lot of drinks and snacks. When I finally arrived I would feel so filthy!

And yet, when I started to think about quitting smoking, I worried about these long car trips. I was afraid that I could never make it through such a long trip without smoking, and that I therefore wouldn't be able to visit my parents again. That's what addiction did to me: it made me scared and dependent. Dependent on smoking. Afraid that without smoking, I couldn't even visit my parents anymore.

In retrospect, that appears to belong to the illusions of the addiction. I still drive to my parents. Sometimes I will be bored during the trip. But I found a new activity: I sing. I belt it out with the radio, or just improvise on signs that can be seen at the side of the road. "Beware of Falling Rocks" and "Click it or Ticket" become blues or country and western tune lyrics. I really believe that I'm less bored during these long drives now than when I still smoked. And when I arrive, I definitely feel a lot fitter and happier than when I still smoked.

Are you also afraid of quitting smoking? That's understandable. That's what addiction does to you: it makes you scared and keeps you from improving the quality of your life. In retrospect, after quitting smoking, you will hardly understand why it took you so long to take the leap. It's great not to have to smoke anymore. Sometimes, I'm still bored. But I'm able to accept it now. Or to do something about it. The choice is mine, and I feel free to choose. Because I'm no longer addicted.

Chapter 12

Smoking In Positive Passive Situations

Positive passive situations are those in which you relax. Relaxing often involves spending time with friends, reading, watching movies, TV or other activities.

How do you feel about the following reasoning?

> Everything that promotes relaxation is good.
>
> Smoking helps me relax.
>
> So smoking must be good.

This seems like a watertight argument. And it is a watertight argument, but the beginning premises aren't correct. It's a smoker's argument. Compare this reasoning with the following:

Every form of compulsion and powerlessness interferes with relaxation.

Smoking is compulsive.

So smoking interferes with relaxation.

Also watertight, isn't it? It's a matter of how you formulate a problem, which starting points you choose, and by using logic you'll come to totally diverging conclusions. Let's change from the philosophical reasoning to a more practical observation of reality. I will start with an example from my own smoking past.

I sing in an amateur choir, and after rehearsal we always go to a bar for some pleasant fellowship. Our rehearsals take place in a church in which noone is permitted to smoke. Most of the other singers start chatting away with each other right after the rehearsal. When I smoked, I couldn't join in the socializing, because I was dying for a cigarette and was disturbed by their dawdling. Thus, the smoking caused the first form of stress. Then we would all go to a bar, and I could finally light up my long-awaited cigarette. Only from that moment on was I able to relax. That is the relaxation caused by smoking: the lessening of the stress that is caused by withdrawal of the previous cigarette. In Graph 5, you will find a representation.

In the graph, the vertical axis is the relaxation axis. The higher the curve, the more relaxed you are. The dotted line shows the relaxation curve of the non-smoker, for example on entering a bar or arriving at a party. Also for

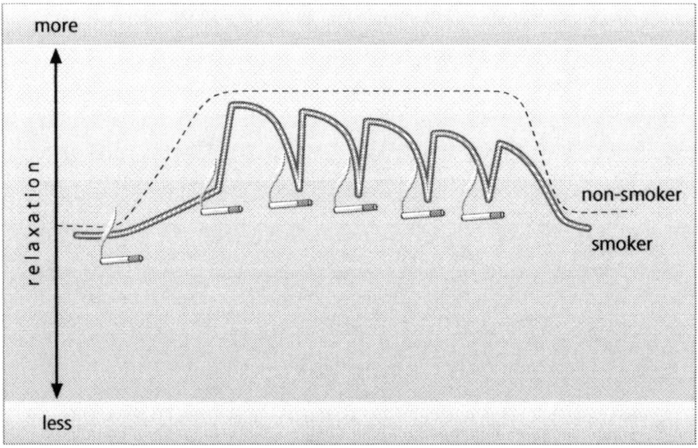

Graph 5: Smoking interferes with relaxation.

a non-smoker, it takes a while before he can truly relax. I assume that the smoker has just smoked a cigarette, so he enters the party without any withdrawal. But while the non-smoker is relaxing more and more, the smokers starts to be bothered by withdrawal. The idea that he needs a cigarette to be able to relax interferes with relaxing. Only after the lighting of a cigarette, the curve of his relaxation rises. But after a while, he feels withdrawal symptoms again, and the relaxation curve goes down again, until he lights a new cigarette. During the entire evening, this pattern repeats itself again and again, and the periods between two cigarettes will become shorter all the time.

With all these so-called relaxing cigarettes, you will never get as relaxed as a non-smoker in the same situation. In the company of non-smokers, you will try not to blow smoke in their faces. After some time, you'll notice that the cigarettes don't taste so good anymore. You'll feel bad because you're smoking more than you like. You try to postpone the next cigarette until after the next round of drinks, but that gives you withdrawal stress. That's how you are imprisoned in the addiction cycle. You're smoking incessantly out of a wish for relaxation and in order not to have to think of smoking all the time, with the result that you're relaxing less and less.

Addiction is like a slippery post. At the top of this post the possibility for relaxation resides, the support for stressful and boring situations. Every cigarette brings you to the top of the post, frees you for a very short time from compulsive thoughts about smoking, and then makes you slide down further in dependency, in addiction. On a daily basis you climb this post dozens of times and then you slide back. Do you like this game? No? Let me tell you a little secret: Nobody is forcing you to keep playing this game. Real freedom is within arm's reach. You only have to let go, of that post to quit this ridiculous addiction game! In order to let go you will need courage, one moment of real courage, in which you choose a happier life. After that, the rest is smooth sailing.

Is quitting smoking hard? Definitely, but only before the moment of quitting.

After quitting there is only relief, freedom, energy, and self-confidence.

Chapter 13

The Smoker Who Gets Out of Control

Every smoker knows these situations in which the smoking gets temporarily but completely out of control. I already told you about my long car trips, in which I smoked like a madman. Also at parties, I would smoke about twice as much as usual. In the previous chapters, the situations in which you smoke were divided into four areas characterized by the factors positive-negative and active-passive. When you consider the circumstances in which you smoke a lot more than usual, you will find that a combination or a quick alternation of several factors characterizes them. The long car trips were mainly characterized by boredom for me, but at the same time I had to keep concentrated on driving as well.

At parties it's not only the matter of relaxation that is involved, but often there's also the factor of stress. Maybe you feel insecure because you don't see a lot of familiar faces. Or maybe you spot a very attractive person. The tension rises, thoughts come up: Shall I start a conversation? How do I look? Should I wait until the other person takes the initiative? Finally, there is another reason to smoke more at parties: Let's be honest, sometimes they're plain boring. You stay because you have nothing better to do. And you smoke out of boredom.

Some people smoke until they're blue in the face during a party game. I used to participate in card games. We would play poker for money. Not even for high amounts, a super successful evening wouldn't amount to more than fifty dollars. But boy, did we smoke on those evenings! Because it was really nice and relaxing. But you also had to concentrate very well to memorize the cards that were already in the game. And at the moment that you're holding a worthless card in your hands, but still bluff a full house with a poker face. What stress! So there were three out of four "smoke-factors" at work.

Are these situations in which you smoke much more than usual also a lot harder after you've quit? The answer is no! When you no longer think and feel like an addict and see smoking through the eyes of a non-smoker, you will know that breathing in smoke contributes nothing to being sociable; it doesn't support you at all in stressful situations; it doesn't make you more self-confident;

and that you will get bored at least just as easily. Of course, you will sometimes still think of smoking in these situations. You will think, "How nice that I don't feel forced to smoke anymore." And you will feel a lot more self-confident.

That's all very well—you will say perhaps—but even if smoking doesn't do anything for me, I still think it tastes good! I won't argue with you about this. Not yet. This is what the next chapter is about.

Are you tired, saturated with information? Then take a break. Smoke a cigarette and try to enjoy it as consciously as possible. Are you fit? Then read on, and be prepared for a minor landslide.

Chapter 14

Smoking Does (Not) Taste Good

This is one of the most difficult chapters. It's hard for me to put into words what I mean exactly. It's hard for you to understand what is almost impossible to understand for a smoker. Before I start, I want to address those smokers who don't enjoy the taste of smoking anymore and who only smoke because they can't refrain from it. This chapter is also for you. Because there has been a time that you did enjoy smoking. And maybe some of all those cigarettes that you smoke still taste a little good to you. The illusion of "tastiness" is one of the most subtle and persistent effects of addiction.

But let's start at the beginning.

There is no accounting for tastes. What is enjoyed by one, is detested by another. There is no such thing as being objective about taste. What tastes good and what tastes bad is mainly determined by the culture you live in and by the way you were raised. There are people in this world who consider the eyes of a cow a delicacy—or the testicles of a dog, or the soft parts of a snail, or the tongue of an ox, or the leg of a pig. It depends on the culture you were raised in. With food, it is pre-eminently the case that the way it tastes is influenced by foreknowledge. That lovely spicy soup you had on your trip to the Far East tasted quite good until the cook told you proudly that the broth was boiled with fresh goat testicles and grasshoppers.

There are also dishes that you have to "learn to eat." Most children don't like Brussels sprouts and chicory, because of their bitter taste. Later in life one learns to appreciate that taste, though the bitterness has to be wrapped in a smoothing cheese—or cream sauce, or linked with savory or sweet tastes. Pure bitterness is actually always an awful taste, but in combination with other tastes it can be enjoyed. Pure bitterness is never enjoyed, because it was originally a warning signal against eating poison.

The body has more of these built-in warning signals. A child who accidentally takes a sip of whiskey will scream from fright and pain, because it leaves a burning feeling on the tongue and in the throat. A child who accidentally inhales smoke will cough vehemently. That's the body's warning signal, pointing out the inferior quality of the inhaled air.

Almost every human being inhaling smoke for the first time will start coughing. Her eyes will water and sometimes she will even feel nauseous. The human respiratory system is not built for inhaling smoke at all. The first cigarettes that you smoke don't taste good. That is, by the way, also the reason that you could become addicted to it. Imagine you would have felt a heavenly intoxication when you smoked your first cigarette, exclaiming "Oh, this is so good!" Then you would have been warned from the start of the danger of becoming addicted.

But that first cigarette was filthy, and the second and third were maybe, as well. And you thought, "This tastes so bad, I'll never get addicted to this." So you smoked once in a while, just to be part of the group, or to socialize or because your parents were against it, or for whatever reason. That's how you gradually became addicted and learned to like the taste of cigarettes. An important factor is that others seemed to like it and that you only really belonged to the group if you liked it as well.

It almost never happens that a first-time smoker actually likes the taste of a cigarette. When he does, there is usually an extra psychological reason for it. One of my clients kept arguing that she had definitely liked the taste of her very first cigarette. She even described it as "the best-tasting cigarette I ever smoked." I asked her to describe the event. She told about her dominant father, whose attitude towards her had always been strict, distant, and contemptuous. One day she revolted against his oppression in a very special way. When he was taking an afternoon nap, she secretly took a cigarette out of his pack and took it to the bathroom. The smoking of this cigarette felt like an act of total defiance and revenge against her father. Of course this cigarette tasted delicious.

I've stated before that the question of a good or a bad taste is determined strongly by psychological factors. It is possible that this first cigarette had such a heavy symbolic meaning for you that your physical defense mechanism was overshadowed by your psychological euphoria. Why does the mind try so hard to make you believe that smoking tastes good?

In the beginning it's only the expectation that it will taste good, because why would all those people keep smoking otherwise? Once you're addicted, you create the illusion that it tastes good. It is, afterall, the only legitimate reason for doing something that otherwise consists only of drawbacks. Why would you pay a lot of money for smoking cigarettes at the expense of your health, your vitality, and your self-respect, if you don't even like the taste of them?!

Smoking has to taste good, because again and again you long desperately for a cigarette, and when you light one this longing disappears for a while. When a yearning is fulfilled, we call that good. With smoking however, this yearning is actually a torment that the "good" cigarette temporarily ends. At the same time, the foundation for the next torment is laid, in the form of a new dose of nicotine in the blood.

Do you take the longest line in the supermarket on purpose, so that it is better when it's finally your turn? Do you look for the highway with the most traffic, because it is so nice to pick up speed after you have been stuck in a traffic jam? Do you deliberately tighten your belt two holes too tight, because it feels so good to loosen it after an hour? Do you deliberately create withdrawal symptoms dozens of times a day, because it feels so good to get rid of them?

That's what's "good" about smoking.

The smoker thinks:

I'M ADDICTED TO SMOKING BECAUSE IT TASTES SO GOOD.

In fact, it's like this:

SMOKING TASTES GOOD BECAUSE I'M ADDICTED.

It's a very distinguishing feature of addiction to learn to love something revolting. Can you imagine that it tastes good to drink thirty cans of beer a day? The alcoholic really enjoys it. Can you imagine that it's good to sniff some sharp white powder through your nose? Try it with flour. I can assure you: it hurts. The cocaine and amphetamine addict really likes it though. Can you imagine that it feels good to stick a needle through your skin into a vein? The heroin junky loves it.

Every addiction appears to have a threshold in the revolting way that the particular device is administered. With other addictions there is an immediate reward behind this threshold, in the form of a stimulating or relaxing high. With smoking, the only "reward" is to be freed of the withdrawal from the previous cigarette.

Let's do an experiment in which you can find out for yourself. I want you to scratch the back of your left hand with your right hand firmly, right away, while you're reading. Keep doing it for about ten seconds. Is that a nice feeling? No, it even hurts a little; it creates a burning sensation. If you had a mosquito bite in that spot, it would have been a nice feeling to scratch. The withdrawal after the smoking of a cigarette can be compared to an itch. The smoking of the next cigarette is the scratching. While you're scratching, you don't feel the itch; that makes the scratching feel good. Question: Does scratching yourself feel good? Answer: Only when you first have an itch. Same question: Does smoking taste good or doesn't it? Answer: Only when you make sure to get some withdrawal first.

You are a smoker. You are addicted, and that's why it's perfectly normal that you enjoy the taste of a cigarette. When you light another cigarette in a while, don't tell yourself: "How stupid, weak, or bad am I to like this." Just think: "What a weird addiction this is, that I even started enjoying the breathing in of smoke." From the first moment on that you've stepped out of your addiction, right from the first day that you quit, you won't like the taste of it anymore. And you will be glad and relieved that you don't have to breathe in smoke anymore in order to feel less bad. To get rid of this yearning to do something that deep in your heart you despise, that's liberation. Why did you think this method is called the Free Yourself Method?

Chapter 15

How Did This Start?

Addiction is a very strange collection of various factors such as dependence, compulsion, illusions, and feelings of guilt. Someone who is addicted rarely asks himself how this addiction came into being. Most smokers think of themselves as stupid, weak, or bad for starting to smoke. But were they? In this chapter we will go back in history.

I want you to go back in your mind to the period in your life in which you started smoking. I don't mean that one cigarette that you secretly smoked as a child with your friends. I mean the period, in which you gradually started smoking more and more, until you couldn't refrain from it anymore. Maybe it was during the time you went to high school, maybe later in college or during the first period of looking for a job. When you want to, close your eyes for a moment after reading this paragraph, and think of the people you were with back then, think of the things you liked and the difficulties that you maybe had. Try to remember how you felt at that time. Were you still an adolescent, with all the insecurity that comes with it? Or was it later, for the first time on your own feet, full of insecurities about life and about yourself?

Addictions almost always start in a period of time in which you're not so self-assured, a time in which you don't have a clear image of your own identity and your future. A lot of people aren't even aware of these difficulties.

I started smoking shortly before my eighteenth birthday, when I had just gone away from home and had my first job in the big city. Only later, I realized how terribly lonely I had been in those years. Back then, I just thought that it was supposed to be that way—that life was joyful when something nice happened to you once in a while, and just lonely the rest of the time. It was so terribly important to belong to a group at that time that I didn't hesitate for a second when the first joints passed by. Cigarettes quickly followed, and also about those there was never a doubt in my mind. I smoked hashish and weed for at least five years before I realized that I didn't really enjoy it. But in the underground scene that

I was in, smoking stuff was about the most important status symbol. I smoked tobacco for twenty-five years, before I realized that it doesn't taste good at all.

So an addiction often arises in a period of insecurity or stress. An important feature of addiction is that it keeps itself alive. An addiction never goes away by itself, not even when your life has become calmer. For ending an addiction, a conscious choice is always needed.

This book shows you how to make that choice. Then it will become clear that for a long time already, smoking doesn't suit you at all anymore, that it's like a relic from the past that you can get rid of in a day, just like that.

Even when your life is still not back in order, or when you happen to just have a difficult period again, you will see that smoking only enhances the difficulties. After quitting, you will only feel amazement about the fact that it took you such a long time to finally do it.

At some point in the past, you became addicted. You started smoking a cigarette once in a while because you needed the feeling of being together with other people so badly. By smoking, you really belonged to the group. Maybe it was a sign of adulthood to you. Think back to that time once again, and realize that in all your innocence you didn't have the slightest clue of what you were getting yourself into.

Were you stupid, bad, or weak? No, it was just "the thing" to do. Now you can see that it brought you illusory benefits and very real harm. Looking back, you can see that it was a mistake to start smoking. This mistake had far-reaching and long lasting-consequences, but it was still just a mistake. We are all human, and as the saying goes, "To err is human."

Later on in this book, you will read how the smoke addiction is being maintained by negative feelings of self-reproach and guilt. Now I want to ask you the following: If someone that you love a lot—your child, your lover, your best friend—makes a mistake and only realizes it later, would you punish him by being angry and full of reproach about this mistake? Or would you give him understanding and support? If you choose the last possibility, why would you treat yourself worse than you treat somebody else? Accept the fact that you became addicted and that you made a mistake. Accept that becoming addicted to nicotine was a mistake that you will correct very soon. Stop condemning yourself for smoking. You don't help yourself with these reproaches. On the contrary, they keep the addiction alive! Look at the child, the youngster, or the insecure person that you were when you walked into the trap of smoke addiction. Quit condemning this mistake and yourself. Look at it with understanding, with compassion, with love. And acknowledge without guilt, without reproach, but with understanding and care: I am addicted.

Only one question remains: Do you want to stay addicted for the rest of your life or do you want to step out of it? That choice is not affected by the addiction itself. That choice is free! Do you choose addiction? Then keep smoking. Stop reading this book and try to enjoy every cigarette. Only go on reading after you've discovered that you can't smoke without being addicted. And that there is no addiction without compulsion and lack of choice. And that it's impossible to feel good with such restrictions placed on yourself.

Do you choose to end the addiction, even if it scares you a lot right now? Do you choose a life without dependence and self-restriction, even if you don't see how yet? Do you choose this because it's actually the only choice you can make? Then read on and discover the remarkable escape route from the prison of addiction.

Chapter 16

Smoking Always Seemed Such a Normal Thing

One of the reasons that it was so easy to become addicted to nicotine is that it has been considered a relatively normal phenomenon in our society. The idea that smoking is a big social problem that needs to be solved has only arisen recently, and is still not considered a problem everywhere yet. Smoking seems such a normal thing, because we are used to the phenomenon from our childhood.

I was born in 1950. In the 50's, over 90 % of all men living in Holland smoked. At birthday parties, the hostess would not only offer drinks and cake, but also a box with various cigarette brands. At receptions, little glasses filled with cigarettes would be sitting next to the snacks. My father smoked the brand "Golden Fiction." (How's that for a name?) The characteristic way in which he would bounce a cigarette on the nail of his thumb before he lit it, to get rid of the loose crumbs of tobacco, is still a vivid memory—even though he quit smoking over thirty-five years ago! After he quit, he promised me a watch if I wouldn't smoke before my eighteenth birthday. But I left home when I was seventeen, insecurities and all. I never earned that watch.

During the Free Yourself Training sessions, I always ask the participants about the smoking habits of their parents. It appears that over 90% of the participants had parents who smoked during the first five years of their lives. The other 10% appear to have had an older brother, sister, or another live-in family member who smoked.

It's a well-known psychological fact that your "matters of course" are formed during the first three to five years of your life. As a matter of course, you learn your language, the way to react to criticism and compliments, how to see yourself in relation to other people, what you are afraid of, etc. What parents say is less important than what they do in this respect. No matter how many times they say that smoking is bad for you and that you are not allowed to ever touch a cigarette, when they smoke, or when you see them smoke in your memory, you conclude: It must be really nice, if they do something that is so bad. Thus, you learn in your earliest years that smoking is a part of adulthood. It might be bad for you, but in spite of that (or maybe even because of that), it tastes very nice. A little bit like sex, also something that was dealt with in negative terms when I was young. With smoking, as well as with sex, I never listened to my parent's advice. It was fortunate for me in the case of sex, but unfortunate in the case of smoking.

Another way, in which smoking is presented to us as a normal thing, is in the media. In older movies the hero regularly lights a cigarette, and the way in which Humphrey Bogart did that, for example, is followed by millions of men. Cigarette commercials are forbidden on television now, but there are still billboards and magazines that promote certain brands. The major cigarette manufacturers in the United States spend over 4.6 billion dollars per year on advertising. With these commercials, something strange is going on.

Commercials are usually used to raise the sales of a certain product. The goals include finding new consumers and competing with other brands. But the most important reason why somebody starts smoking can't be found in commercials. You start smoking because others smoke and you want to be a part of their group. Commercials play a minor role in this process, and they are only effective where they stress this "becoming a member of the group" effect.

The second major goal of advertisement, competing with other brands, has hardly any effect either. Every smoker knows that once he is used to a certain brand, he will seldom switch to another. In the twenty-five years that I smoked, I smoked three or four different brands at the most. So why do they spend these 100 million bucks on each year?

Let's take a look at the content of cigarette commercials. The values promoted usually include a sense of adventure, power, courage, health, youthfulness, attractiveness, independence, and feeling good. Now, place these values next to the feelings that every smoke addict knows—feelings that are a direct result of smoking.

Advertisement links smoking to:	*The smoker experiences:*
Sense of adventure	Hopelessness
Power	Weakness
Courage	Fear
Health	Being unhealthy
Youthfulness	Decay
Attractiveness	Feeling filthy and repulsive
Independence	Dependence
Feeling good about yourself	Hating yourself

In these oppositions, we can find the most important reason for spending millions on advertisement for cigarettes, more important than finding new smokers and competing with other brands. The most important goal is to keep all those smokers addicted.

Every smoker experiences the drawbacks of smoking on a daily basis. Advertisement compensates these negative emotions a little. Of course we modern, intelligent, liberated people laugh about this macho cowboy who, after he branded the cattle, drinks his coffee and lights his tough cigarette. Of course, we know that it is a paid actor who calms down with a cigarette after controlling a dangerous current in the jungle. But did you think that "understanding how it works" would protect you against the effects of such a commercial? Did you think that those tobacco dealers spend all that money just to give you a good laugh once in a while?

Of course, they know that people can see through their methods of advertising. It doesn't matter; the images and their suggestions will have their effect anyway. The suggestive positive content of the commercial keeps the misconception of a lot of smokers alive. The misconception that smoking tastes good, that it creates a feeling of togetherness, that even as a smoker you can feel strong and healthy and that even as a smoker you can feel free.

Be honest with yourself when you think about the following question. For how long do you already think in the back of you head: I wish I could only smoke a few cigarettes a day, only those that really taste good, and that I could refrain from the other ones? Well, every time you see a commercial about a smoker who is totally satisfied with his life, with himself, with smoking, the illusion is kept alive that it is possible to be happy with smoking. Every time you see some advertisement in which somebody who appears to feel really free smoking at the same time, the illusion is kept alive that it is possible to be a free, not addicted smoker.

If you would be really free to light or not light a cigarette—or to put it differently, if you would not be addicted to smoking—would you smoke those three or four cigarettes a day? Of course not: for someone that is not addicted, cigarettes are filthy. Why would you do something filthy, if only three or four times a day! Smoking only appears to taste good when you are addicted, because it frees you from compulsive thinking of smoking, because it helps you getting rid of the creeping withdrawal symptoms.

But when you don't have those compulsive thoughts, when you don't feel any tormenting craving, in short when you are no longer addicted, than you will feel the difference between the phony values of the tobacco commercials and your own authentic feelings. Then you will feel really strong and independent and healthy and vital.

Some time ago, I saw an ad for tobacco that had the line with capital letters: NO CAGE, NO HERD. When you have stepped out of the cage of addiction, when you have your independent judgment on smoking again, you will see the wry humor of this ad. It reminds me of the motto above the entrance of the concentration camp Auschwitz: "Arbeit macht frei" (work frees you). I don't think this comparison is overdone, nor an expression of too little respect for the six million victims of Nazi Germany. Did you know that worldwide even more than six million people die every year because of smoking? Apart from that, this comparison is faulty of course. There is a big difference between being destroyed by others or destroying yourself. No matter how tragic all those victims of smoking might be, it is their own responsibility. But the fact that commercials are still being made for this creeping form of self-destruction is very cynical indeed. For people who spend their last months in the Mayo Clinic, as well as for their families, the tobacco advertisement must be very bitter.

Chapter 17

The Advantages of Being Addicted

Are there any advantages in being addicted? That depends on how you look at it. Objectively speaking, or rather from the point of view of someone who is not addicted, being addicted doesn't have any advantages. Nobody would ever weigh out the pros and cons of addiction, in order to finally decide to become addicted for a while. In a way, being addicted has certain advantages for the addict. It can be useful to know how you hold on to these seeming advantages, consciously, but very often also unconsciously. But let's start at the beginning.

When you started smoking, cigarettes gave you the advantage of "belonging to the group." For some, smoking was a sign of independence, an act of resistance against parents, or the giving in to a sense of adventure. These advantages disappeared as soon as you found out that you were addicted. Also, because of the growing anti-smoking sentiment in our society, this ”belonging to the group” changes more and more into “not belonging to the group anymore.”

As soon as the addiction is a fact, the “starting advantages” fade, but some new advantages of addiction come into being. In previous chapters, the placebo effect of smoking was already pointed out. This makes smoking look like something that enhances concentration, dispels boredom, helps fight stress and that helps you to relax and have a good time. We know by now these effects only seem to happen, and that in reality the opposite happens. In reality, smoking breaks concentration, disturbs relaxation, enhances stress and makes you feel worse when you’re bored. So this means that we are dealing with an illusion here, the opposite of reality. Let’s take a closer look at the illusions caused by addiction.

The cornerstone of addiction is the illusion that smoking feels good. Or to be more precise: It seems as if your mood improves by smoking. But as we have seen, the cigarette only relieves the torment of withdrawal. It frees you only from compulsive thoughts about smoking. Smoking a cigarette doesn’t make you feel better, it makes you feel less bad.

This illusion of improving your mood has another advantage. It gives the illusion of controlling your mood.

It's easy: You're sad and a cigarette makes you a little bit less sad. You feel nervous and scared, and a cigarette comforts you. You feel tense and a cigarette takes away part of the stress. So you have a magic trick that improves your mood in several seconds!

This control over your mood is the big apparent advantage of the addiction. That's why addictions often start in a period of insecurity, with a lot of mood changes. You feel like a toy, at the mercy of your own emotions. And there is the cigarette that helps you to control your own moods. "A little grip in an uncertain world," is how a lot of smokers come to see the cigarette as a supporting friend, a faithful pal that will always be there for them.

What an absurd comparison, when we look at the real effects of nicotine! Imagine a real buddy. When you're in pain, he relieves it. When you're fighting with friends, he mediates and creates peace. When you're afraid, he protects you. But one day, you find out the horrible truth: The friend that relieves your pain also is the cause of your troubles by poisoning you behind your back. It's your faithful buddy who sets your friends against you before he makes peace with them again. It's your own pal who causes fear, before he protects you against it. Would you stay friends with this person knowing that his two-sided behavior is very slowly killing you?

I must admit, this example sounds a bit dramatic: the so-called best friend, trying to destroy you behind your back. But for 430,700 Americans a year, it is a fact: They die at the hands of their pal, their supportive friend, their buddy.

In uncertain times, you hold on to the illusion of being in control of your own mood changes. That's the apparent advantage of the addiction. But a horrible truth is hidden behind this advantage. It is hidden very well, so you have to look very carefully. This disadvantage becomes visible, when you see your own behavior as an expression of the way you look at yourself. Because each time that you try to free yourself from your insecurities by smoking a cigarette, you are actually, without knowing it, telling yourself: "I am too insecure to handle this situation by myself." Each time that you have to light a cigarette in order to cope with a tense situation, you are telling yourself: "I am too nervous, too weak to cope with this situation without help."

A cigarette gives the illusion of control over your moods, but in reality your freedom is being curbed more and more. Every time you use your addiction to cope with a difficult situation, you are telling yourself: "I can't handle this situation on my own." Every time you use an illusion to handle problems or insecurities, you weaken yourself and therefore deepen the problems.

With other addictions, this effect is a lot easier to see. With an alcoholic or a heroin addict for example, it's obvious: The addiction started to help coping with certain problems, but after a while these problems only got bigger. The addict loses his friends, becomes isolated, and ends up being a wreck. With smoking addiction, the effect—although less visible—is the same. Smoking is a means to compensate insecurity and dependency, which in the end only makes this insecurity and dependency worse.

Every time you feel insecure or bored, or when you have to concentrate, there's this compulsion to light a cigarette. At that moment, you feel powerless. This powerlessness enhances the feeling of being a victim, a victim of your addiction. And this also has a hidden advantage. A victim can blame someone else. All the difficulties caused by neurotic parents, an egotistical lover, difficult children, a lousy job, are enough to make anyone smoke. You need another cigarette to overcome all the set-backs in your life—or so you think.

Each time you are in trouble, or heading towards a difficult situation, as a victim you will feel powerless and dependent. You tell yourself, "It's wiser to wait a little before quitting smoking." You plan to quit as soon as your life is a little smoother again. But once it is smoother, you are much better capable of pushing away troublesome thoughts and feelings. You feel fairly happy, only not about your smoking, but you don't have to think about that now, do you?

That's how being a victim provides a perfect reason to keep smoking. An addiction stays alive by inducing fear for everything that smells like independence. Fear for everything that looks like self-assurance, fear for all the effects of quitting.

The biggest advantage of your addiction is that it keeps you small—dependent instead of independent, a victim of your own past instead of responsible for your own life in the present. But what on earth is the advantage in that, you may ask? Well, here it comes: It is safe and familiar! All our lives, we feel like a victim, it is safe to be able to blame someone else, and we are already so used to this mediocre feeling, to this easy middle road between happiness and unhappiness. Yes, addiction has a big advantage. It's the advantage of mediocrity. It's the advantage of not facing our fears, the advantage of being able to avoid living.

Here we have the deepest hidden and most gruesome advantage of smoking: It slowly ends the life that we didn't feel up to when we started smoking. In that way, the choice to quit smoking is the choice for life itself. Maybe you thought that you had already made this choice for life or that you never had to make this choice. Think again.

To conclude of this chapter, I will share a part of the inaugural speech of Nelson Mandela in 1994. For no special reason, just for your consideration.

Our deepest fear is not that we are inadequate.
Our deepest fear is that we are powerful beyond measure.
It is our light, not our darkness, that frightens us most.
We ask ourselves, who am I to be brilliant, gorgeous, talented and fabulous?
Actually, who are you not to be?

You are a child of God, your playing small doesn't serve the world.
There's nothing enlightened about shrinking so other people won't feel insecure around you.
We are born to make manifest the glory of God that's within us.
It's not just in some of us, it's in everyone.
And as we let our light shine, we unconsciously give other people permission to do the same.
As we are liberated from our own fear, our presence automatically liberates others.

Chapter 18

The Fear of Quitting: Afraid to Fail

Smokers, who begin to think about quitting, often get caught in the middle of two opposite fears. On the one hand, there is the fear of failing in your attempt to quit. And as soon as you get over that one a little bit, the fear arises that you will succeed in your attempt and that you will have do without cigarettes for the rest of your life. A lot of smokers don't see a way out of these double and paradoxical fears, so they will try not to think of quitting at all anymore. These two contradictory fears will be discussed in this chapter, and in the next one.

The fear of failing in your attempt to quit is the direct result of the misconception that it's very hard to quit smoking. Every smoker knows how hard it is to be in a situation in which it is not permitted to smoke, or in which it is impossible to smoke. How hard it must be then, not to be able to smoke at all anymore, for good! The misconception lies in the idea that it is harder to never smoke again than to refrain from smoking for an hour or a day. The opposite is true. It is much, much easier to never smoke again than to temporarily refrain from it. Why? Because in the latter case, you remain an addict, who is deprived of his cigarette. Never to smoke again is much easier, because first you get out of the addiction, after which you simply don't need a cigarette anymore.

Before making the decision to step out of the addiction, the fear of failing takes a prominent place in the smoker's head. A lot of smokers are afraid of losing face with friends and colleagues. "Everybody will know how weak I am for not being able to quit," is the thought that belongs to that fear. But the fear goes deeper than that. Even worse than the loss of face with peers, is the loss of face with yourself. Having to admit to yourself that you didn't succeed in quitting while you wanted to so badly, is hard to swallow. This tough confrontation with your own weakness, your own lack of willpower, this bitter disappointment that you weren't able to free yourself from this oppressing addiction—that's the essential part of the fear of failing in your attempt to quit.

Let's take a closer look at this fear of feeling like a failure. This feeling is not only tied to a failed attempt to quit. With the lighting of every cigarette that you don't really feel like smoking, with every cigarette that doesn't taste good, with every cigarette you smoke in the company of non-smokers, with every cigarette that makes you dizzy or that gives you a coughing fit, in short, with almost every cigarette you smoke, you have this feeling of doing something that you don't really approve of, of being a weakling, of despising yourself a little bit. It's comparable to the financial side of smoking. Every day this addiction costs money, but it's so little that it's easy to forget about. All the same, in the last ten years you might have spent ten thousand dollars on smoking.

In the same way you can forget about your daily "failure feelings," but in several years the damage can run up considerably. The fear of failure of an attempt to quit is, in fact, the fear of a confrontation with this "ran up" account. Still, you can pay this bill once and for all. That's what happens when you ultimately step out of your addiction.

The pushing aside of these daily, subtle "failure feelings" has another disadvantage. These repressed negative feelings will have their influence on an unconscious level. Without noticing, you're developing an attitude towards decisions, hard choices, and challenges that is characterized by a mentality of "it will be extremely hard and I will probably not succeed." This will result in a behavioral pattern of avoiding difficult decisions.

Think about what it could do for you, to stop calling yourself weak dozens of times a day. To stop feeling like the prisoner of your own indecisiveness several times a day.

So the fear of failing in quitting is the fear of temporarily losing your defense mechanism against the feeling of being a worthless weakling. Yet there is something good in this negative judgment about yourself: When you think you are weak for doing something, this means that you feel this action is below your own standards. As long as you still feel weak about lighting a cigarette, you are not. As long as you can't resign yourself to being addicted, as long as you feel resistance inside against this curtailing of your freedom, you still haven't lost your self-esteem. It is because of this feeling of self-esteem that you long for an escape from your addiction.

This fear of failing to quit is fear of a confrontation with yourself. In fact, it is a normal human phenomenon to be afraid of failure when facing a difficult challenge. In the case of an addiction, this fear takes on enormous proportions. The addiction makes you feel weak and powerless against the compulsive nature of smoking. We're looking at another typical "addiction-inversion" of reality. The smoker thinks, "I'm staying addicted because I am a weakling." In reality, you feel like a weakling because you are addicted, and you will feel powerless as long as you stay addicted.

Because of this feeling, it's almost impossible to imagine that you could succeed in quitting smoking.

The extreme fear belongs to the addiction, and will end as soon as you step out of the addiction. This fear of failing is one of the treacherous mechanisms that the addiction uses to stay alive. Let's take a look at how this mechanism works.

Someone who feels fear will try to make herself feel more secure. That's a normal phenomenon, on which insurance companies depend for example (which doesn't necessarily mean that every insurance policy originates in fear). With quitting smoking, this fear has disastrous consequences. Someone who quits smoking and secures oneself against the fear of failing, secures the failure. How will this happen? Some smokers will keep their attempt to quit a secret, to prevent loss of face if they fail. They are saying, in fact, that it's a stupid idea to try to quit, except when you succeed. What nonsense! Every attempt to escape this psychologically undermining and physically debilitating addiction is a positive action. Why would you be ashamed of that? This is what addiction is doing to you; it is making you weak.

Other smokers do the opposite when they try to quit. They tell everybody about it, they make bets, they make promises to themselves and others. Their intention is to let the fear of losing face help them stay away from cigarettes when the craving gets bad. What do you mean, craving? When you've stepped out of the addiction, you won't like smoking at all anymore. Besides, there is a strange twist in this construction. You try to brace yourself against the fear of failure by making this fear extra big. It's obvious that the effect will be contrary, because you're putting yourself in a situation in which you are not allowed to smoke on penalty of being ridiculed. As long as you tell yourself that you are not allowed to smoke, smoking will stay a temptation and you will make quitting unnecessarily difficult.

There is another reason why the fear of failing in your attempt to quit will maintain your addiction. This is related to the misconception that failure is worse when the attempt was more serious. Most attempts to quit will therefore be clothed in escape clauses. For example: "I hope that I won't put on too much weight, because I'd rather be a slender smoker than a fat non-smoker." Or, "If I can't do my work without smoking, I will start again. I have to provide for my family." These kinds of escape routes serve to limit loss of face in case of failure. They serve to legitimize failure. And that's how they increase the possibility of failure. What is worse, failing after a half-hearted attempt, or failing after you've been giving yourself one hundred percent? Fear will whisper in your ear that failing after giving yourself fully is worse. The disappointment seems worse in that case and the loss of face the most painful. If you fail after a half-hearted attempt, you can at least tell yourself that you will succeed the next time, because you will try harder then. And you're back in the cycle of addiction again. For that's one of the features of addiction: to have the intention to quit some day. That's how the addiction maintains itself. It is fear that brings about these half-hearted attempts. In reality, the opposite is true: The more you dedicate yourself to achieve a goal, the less painful it will be to fail.

Let me explain with an example: Compare quitting smoking to the climbing of the highest peak in the Himalayas, Mount Everest. That would probably scare a lot of smokers less than quitting smoking. Imagine the leader of the expedition being interviewed, after failing to reach the summit. "How do you feel now, Mr. Mountaineer, are you very disappointed?" The answer goes, "Well, it is a pity of course, but the disappointment isn't very severe, because we didn't have enough oxygen cylinders anyway, and we also didn't prepare fully for climbing without oxygen. No, actually, we were very well prepared for failure."

Do you see how bizarre it is to cover yourself for failure like this? The failing of a plan is always disappointing. But if you have done everything that's in your power, if you have given 100 percent of yourself, then you can look yourself straight in the eye and wish yourself better luck next time.

In one respect, this comparison doesn't work. With climbing Mount Everest, there are countless mitigating factors that can jeopardize the success of the undertaking. With quitting smoking there are no mitigating factors at all. If you try half-heartedly, you can be practically sure of failure. If you give everything you have, including your fear of failing, you can be absolutely sure of success. In that case you will be freed from smoking for good, on the day you finish this book! And you'll be freed from the fear of failure, too.

Chapter 19

The Fear of Quitting: Afraid to Succeed

After you've more or less accepted the fear of failure, the idea of quitting often brings about a new fear. This is the fear that you will succeed in your attempt. Ahead of you lies this big, black void of a life without cigarettes. "How can I lead my life from then on? There will be no more fun; I will hardly be able to concentrate at all; every stressful situation will turn into a disaster; during long car trips I will be bored to death, and for the rest of my life I will miss that tasty cigarette after dinner and with my coffee." That's how the fear of a life without smoking looks, only much, much worse....

In previous chapters, we saw how nicotine is not responsible for increasing concentration, relieving boredom or stress, or allowing one to relax. But one the scariest mental hurdles for smokers trying to quit is the idea of having no more fun smoking and far less sociability. A lot of smokers feel that smokers are much more sociable than non-smokers. That's easily accounted for. For with whom do you go outside to smoke a cigarette during the intermission of a meeting? And who never complains about the smell of your cigarettes? Every smoker feels more or less guilty about smoking. But in the company of other smokers, this feeling is easy to repress. They do it, too, so why bother?

This little detour brings us back again to the good feeling of "belonging to a group." Smoking together with others, especially in an environment in which nobody smokes, creates a feeling of togetherness. It's not nice to feel like a weakling, but together with others who feel like weaklings too, it seems less bad. This feeling of togetherness is another illusion. Nothing, absolutely nothing, would remain of this togetherness, if it wasn't for the smoking. It's the addiction that creates the illusion of togetherness, and because of that it prevents real togetherness.

It's a fortunate circumstance that smoking isn't forbidden in our society, and that cigarettes aren't too expensive. Otherwise, every cigarette addict might start to steal, cheat and rob others in order to get his cigarettes. Addicts can be ruthless. The compulsive thoughts of smoking are stronger than any other thoughts. Togetherness is the most ironic illusion of every addiction. Do you think your smoking friends will come and visit you when you are at the Mayo Clinic? Maybe you do have good friends that you smoke with. But if they are real friends, they are so in spite of smoking, not because of it.

Time flies when you're having fun. When you are enjoying yourself, you lose track of time. When you lose yourself in a nice book, you forget the time. In a lot of different situations, the feeling of time can disappear. "Gee, is it that late already?", you will say surprised, and that always means that you totally lost yourself in what you were doing. To "lose yourself" in something is an experience of happiness.

Time flies when you're having fun. This isn't true for the smoke addict. The addiction has a biological clock that starts ticking after extinguishing a cigarette. After a quarter of an hour, give or take a minute, withdrawal symptoms appear. It's like an alarm that's going off, quietly at first, then louder and louder, until you have to turn it of by lighting the next cigarette. Of course, smokers can also lose themselves in activities too, but not for very long. Once in a while, you relapse because of the withdrawal alarm that's going off. You light another cigarette, after which you can do whatever you want again for some time. No matter how much they enjoy what they are doing, smokers take a break much more often than non-smokers. They are forced to turn off the withdrawal alarm. That's why you smoke so much even while working on something you like. That's why you smoke so much during a nice get together.

Does smoking add to the atmosphere? For a smoke addict this seems to be true. The smoke addict cannot give himself up to sociability without first lighting a cigarette. I will give you an example from my own smoking past.

I only really liked smoking when I could drink something with it: coffee, soda, or a glass of port wine. As soon as I would sit down on the pavement of a cafe with some friends, they would immediately start chatting away (right: non-smokers). I would mainly feel like smoking and would look around for the waiter. Also after the orders were taken, I would keep looking around, waiting impatiently for my drink. If it took a while, I would become irritated. I would hardly be capable of joining the conversation until finally the cappuccino was being served, and I could smoke my cigarette. I only started to be sociable after lighting a cigarette. Did this cigarette cause the nice atmosphere? No, it was already there, but I couldn't enjoy it before turning off my withdrawal alarm. And often I would fall back outside of the togetherness. Each time that I needed a cigarette and annoyed myself for smoking too quickly or too much, I would "remove" myself from the nice atmosphere.

So smoking is not a means to create a nice atmosphere; smoking is a necessity for enjoying it. If you are addicted, that is. Only an addict has to light a cigarette every half hour, or even more often, in order to be able to fully enjoy the nice atmosphere. It seems as if you enjoy those cigarettes. In reality you are enjoying the nice atmosphere, not the cigarette. Or more precise: you are enjoying the taking away of the blockade between you and the nice atmosphere. Without that cigarette you are not even capable anymore of enjoying yourself. That's what addiction does to you. It turns everything around, so that you are even afraid of being freed from the compulsion to smoke.

Do you think that the atmosphere in your life will never be nice anymore after quitting smoking? The opposite is true. You will be capable of enjoying nice times in a lot more situations and for a lot longer at a time. You won't have to smoke in order to be able to relax anymore. You won't have to smoke in order to be able to join in some fun anymore. You don't have to slowly destroy yourself in order to be able to enjoy life anymore.

It is very understandable that you feel this fear for a life without smoking. This fear belongs to being addicted. But this book is actually not about quitting smoking, but about quitting being addicted. From the moment that you decide to get out of this confining addiction, your fear will change into happiness, the confinement into freedom. I can't give you anything that makes the fear disappear before you make this decision. But you have something to set against this fear: desire. Do you desire a life without addiction, without fears, without confinement, without guilt, without self-reproach, without dizziness, coughing fits, and bad odors? Then enjoy this desire. Let the fear be. Don't try to push it away, because it is part of being addicted. Instead look forward to a future without the misery of smoking. You are almost there!

Chapter 20

The Myth of Self-Conquest

How should you do something that scares you a lot? You already have been reading several chapters about fear being a part of addiction, but how to overcome this fear? Maybe there are more situations in your life that scare you. Are you afraid to criticize people or to stick up for yourself? When a friend acts in a way that you don't agree with, are you afraid of telling him? When somebody doesn't wait her turn at the counter of a crowded store, do you say something about it? There are so many situations in life that make us a little nervous or afraid. Very often, we try to avoid situations like that. Let's take a closer look at fears like that.

The fear that I am talking about is a different kind of fear than the one you experience when you feel threatened, like with a traffic violation or when you are facing a painful doctor's examination. The fear of quitting smoking, of being honest to others, of being assertive, is always the fear of rejection. This fear is connected to a desire. You desire to be freed from your addiction and you fear failure. You long for the understanding of others and you fear that they won't extend it. You long for justice and you're afraid of being treated unjustly.

Why are we so afraid of rejection? This has to do with the first years of our life, in which rejection is a daily recurring phenomenon. Babies usually ask more than parents can give. Some parents are capable of rejecting in a loving fashion. Others reject in an irritated fashion. The difference depends, among other things, on the way they were rejected by their parents. A loving rejection of a child who's whining for an ice cream cone would sound more or less like this: "You will not get an ice cream cone and I don't like it when you're whining." The irritated rejection sounds like, "You're such a nuisance! You won't get an ice cream cone." In the first case, the parent says, "I don't like your behavior." In the other case, "I don't like you." In the first case, the child learns to correct a certain behavior; in the second, he experiences rejection or judgment.

I explained already that our "matters of course" are formed in the first years of our lives. If you look at the fact that no parents are ideal and that every child gets some irritated reactions from them, you will understand why all people are more or less afraid of being rejected. It's rejection that gives us back these deep-rooted feelings of our childhood, feelings of not being okay, of being bad or worthless.

Let's take another look at the situation in which a friend of yours does or says something that you don't agree with, or that irritates you. You think about saying something about it, but you feel insecure or even afraid to do so. How will your friend react? Will he get angry and reject you? Or will you make him sad, so that you will feel guilty? Thus, your fear looks ahead at the possibility of rejection by the other. There are two possibilities now. The first one is to keep your mouth shut, thinking, "Well, it's not that bad. It's just the way he is. I probably shouldn't get myself all worked up about it." You don't feel comfortable with this decision. You feel a little bit weak, perhaps a little similar to the feeling you have when you light a cigarette in the presence of non-smokers. By succombing to the fear of rejection, you are ultimately rejecting yourself.

The second possibility is to tell your friend what you feel about what he did or said, not to judge him, but just to be honest and to express your feelings. If you want, you can add that you are nervous about saying this, and that he should decide for himself what he does with your remark. Most likely, your friend will respect you for your honesty, and communication between the two of you will be totally open. But also, if your friend turns away from your remark, or gets angry even, it will be obvious that he's the one with a problem, not you.

Are you a person who has no difficulties in being honest with friends? Then imagine a situation in which you want to tell your parents that you love them in spite of everything. Or take the situation in which you want to tell your partner that you've slept with somebody else. Everybody knows situations in which there is a fear of rejection. If you surrender to that fear, avoiding the risk of rejection, you will reject yourself and feel worthless.

The fear to fail quitting smoking is a double fear of rejection. There is the fear that others will think you are a weakling and above all that you will feel that you are a weakling yourself. But in avoiding this fear, you will also feel like a weakling, with every cigarette that you light. That's a characteristic feature of addiction: whatever direction you look, there is always fear. Fear of staying addicted, fear of quitting. The question is: How can one overcome this fear? The answer is simple and seemingly disappointing: Fear should not be conquered. It's not even beyond doubt that fear can ever be conquered. Maybe you can deny it, by screaming loudly that you are not afraid, by drinking a lot of alcohol, by numbing your feelings. This method won't work though, especially not with quitting smoking. You shouldn't conquer fear; you should embrace it and take it with you.

A lot of people use their fears as warning signs: WATCH OUT, STAY AWAY, DON'T DO THIS, OR AVOID THIS SITUATION. Whole areas of their lives are fenced off with these signs. Their living space gets smaller and smaller. The feeling of being a prisoner gets stronger and stronger. And all because they interpret their fears in the wrong way! Fears are not warning signs, rather they are indicators. They indicate the route to freedom, to honesty, to independence, to enjoying your life. It's a big misconception that you have to conquer your fear in order to be able to do what you were afraid of. As a matter of fact, you should first do what you are afraid of, whereupon your fear will change into a feeling of freedom and self-respect.

In all religious and mythological stories, we can find the themes of fear and victory. Jesus of Nazareth was afraid the evening he was arrested on the Mount of Olives. Did he conquer his fear? No, he gave up resisting his fear and found peace with himself and his destiny. The hobbit Frodo from *Lord of the Rings* was terrified when he ascended Mount Mordor in order to throw the ring into the fire. He even knew that he wouldn't survive, but the goal was more important. In the end, he did survive, or rather, there was a new and purified life for him. The same transpires for Indiana Jones, who had to step from a cliff into a deep chasm in *The Temple of Doom*. His fear of crashing wasn't conquered at all, but his belief that the right path was in front of him was greater than his fear.

He stepped into the unfathomable depths and found the way to the Holy Grail—after which everything collapses with a lot of bangs in a big finale, because that's the way it goes in a modern adventure movie.

There are thousands of examples like these. Are they all just nice bedtime stories? I think this theme appeals to us because it is, in fact, the theme of every human life. On the one hand, there's the fear that slows us down, paralyzes us, and drags us down, as long as we fight it. On the other hand, there is the ideal, the deep desire for freedom, beauty, honesty, and love. As soon as we stop fighting our fear, as soon as we stop avoiding it, but embrace it and use it as a force in the direction of good, we will find freedom from fear and the fulfillment of our desires.

For me, quitting smoking, definitely and for good, was a real heroic adventure. I felt like a hero the first day after the decision to quit. The fear disappeared; I felt freed from an oppressive addiction and was very happy and relieved. Since then, I've started doing other things that scare me. Why not? When you step out of a twenty-five-year-old smoking addiction in one day, you feel that you are capable of just about anything.

That's exactly the secret of fear. It seems as if it tells you, "Look out, you can't do that; that won't work; don't try; run away." In fact, fear tells you, "This is where you want to go. Here lies an expansion of your happiness." Go figure: Have you ever been afraid of piloting a four-engine jumbo jet by yourself? No, it probably never even occurred to you to do such a thing. (The reader who has been afraid of flying a jumbo jet is probably already a pilot on such a machine.) The things that scare you are the things you are capable of doing. They are the things that you want, that suit you, that will expand your boundaries, and enrich your life. That's why you are so afraid of quitting smoking, because you know that you can do it! It's a confrontation with your own power, so no matter how badly you want to be freed of your addiction, it's scary to have to give up your life as an addict in order find a new life as a free human being. It's the fear that will function as a door to a freer, better and cleaner life. Don't fight that fear, but go through it, and fill yourself with the longing for a life without addiction. It is such a good feeling to be freed from smoking.

Chapter 21

Health

The subject of health is a sensitive one for smokers. I promise that in this chapter I won't start telling gruesome stories about all kinds of horrible diseases. I also won't give you scary pictures or descriptions of what the lungs of a smoker look like. Not out of consideration for your feelings, but because such an approach works counterproductively.

Often, I get clients who recently received some bad news from their doctor. There was this man in his fifties who had heard that his heart didn't function well anymore. If he didn't quit smoking, he would probably be gone within half a year. This man told me that he had started smoking a lot more since his doctor told him this. He was desperate.

Then there was this woman in her forties, a mother of three children, who knew that if she didn't quit smoking, her legs would be amputated within a year. She smoked almost double the amount of what she usually smoked and was close to a nervous breakdown.

Smokers who know that soon they are going to be confronted with some serious consequences of smoking, will usually start smoking more. I have heard other smokers, who aren't threatened by a deadly disease, saying things like, "I wish a doctor would give me a big fright, then I would be able to quit." Well, forget about it. The bigger the fear of physical consequences of smoking, the more difficult it is to quit. How does this strange mechanism work?

Every smoker knows the feeling. You get it with a bad smoker's coughing fit, or when you suddenly hear a little wheeze in your throat while you're talking, or when you are dizzy from the first cigarette in the morning, or when somebody else is talking about your health. In short, the feeling of guilt you feel for injuring your own health. But at the same time, you feel the craving for a cigarette. Because of that, you feel even more guilty: How can you crave something that is so bad for your health? The longing for a cigarette intensifies the sense of guilt. You want to get rid of this sense of guilt. So what do you do? You light a cigarette. This cigarette frees you from the craving for a cigarette for a while and thus from some of the guilty feelings. At least during the smoking of that cigarette, you can tell yourself that soon you will really quit.

What happens when the doctor tells you that things will really go wrong with you in the near future? At that moment, it's your dearest wish to quit smoking. But at the same time you feel this craving for a cigarette. You know that this cigarette constitutes your death, or the loss of both your legs. So what do you feel? Guilt and self-reproach! You feel guilty for craving something that is disastrous for your health. The compulsive thought, that you need a cigarette, creates a sense of guilt and powerlessness. You want to get rid of these bad feelings as soon as possible, so what do you do? You light another cigarette. For one moment, your thoughts are at peace. For one moment, it is possible to think about your painful situation and make plans to quit. For one moment, you feel a little bit less guilty. But soon the next withdrawal will start again, and you will start to feel guilty again. With each cigarette, this feeling grows, and you will become more and more powerless.

The vicious cycle of addiction has become a vortex that takes you down at high speed. It seems impossible to ever escape this deadly addiction. The stronger the feelings of guilt, the more you dislike yourself. The weaker you feel, the further away you seem to be from the way out. That's what addiction does to you: It creates the illusion that there is no way to escape. Break through this illusion! Stop with these senseless feelings of guilt! Take off those addiction glasses! Break with this horrible addiction, for once and for all. It is the only way out and a very beautiful one. The deeper the misery is from which you escape, the greater the joy over the regained freedom. You will truly be able to start a new life.

Some smokers, who have already smoked for thirty or forty years or even longer, are afraid that it's already too late for them to quit smoking. They think that they already have cancer and that it doesn't matter for them anymore if they quit or not. However, statistics tell us that after ten years of non-smoking, the life expectancy of the ex-smoker is the same as that of the non-smoker. So, even if you are eighty or even older, quitting smoking immediately reduces the chances of big physical troubles in the future.

But a lot more important is the immediate improvement of your condition when you quit smoking. Within three weeks after quitting, your condition has already improved 15 to 20 per cent. You can really feel that! Within several days you already get more air, and that's a great feeling. Also your immune system will improve very quickly. The idea that smokers have a cold less often than non-smokers is absolutely nonsensical. Smokers have a permanently stuffed nose, and they rattle and cough all day long. You don't only quit to prevent diseases in the future, but mainly to become healthier right after quitting and to feel more fit and vital.

A lot of smokers have found a way to get rid of their guilty feelings about smoking. They know that every smoker has a chance of one in four to die from lung cancer or a heart or vascular disease. "So," they say happily, "there is a chance of three in four that I won't get cancer!" This is the typical reasoning of an addict. Would you cross a busy road with a blindfold on if chances would be one in four that you wouldn't reach the other side alive? Besides, there is another fallacy in this reasoning. Of course, the chance that you will die of a smoking-related disease is "only" one in four. But that doesn't mean that in three out of four cases nothing will go wrong. In fact, smoking shortens the lives of all smokers, by breaking down the immune system as a consequence of a decreased absorption of oxygen in the blood. You just don't know for how long you would have lived otherwise. But really, all this juggling with numbers and chances is tiresome. It's like bargaining with the most precious possession you have—your health.

Let's not try to fool anybody. Quitting smoking in order not to get cancer later in life is nonsense. You could be run over by a cab before that time. And also, non-smokers can get cancer or other horrible diseases. For some of us—smokers and non-smokers—life holds some huge difficulties in store, and it is usuless to be afraid in advance. Still, this kind of misery is more difficult for smokers than for non-smokers. Imagine some time in the far future. You've just had a talk with the doctor at your hospital bed. He had some bad news for you. That's horrible enough, no matter if you smoke or not. But imagine the devastating insecurity that you will have as a smoker, that this was all unnecessary. All this misery could have been avoided! Can you imagine your regrets when you look at your past, when you still could have changed your fate? Imagine the shame you will feel facing the people who love you? How badly you would wish to change your past, to make another choice. But it is irrevocably too late.

Enough about this! Away with this black shadow that looms over the future. It is not too late at all! You can choose another life. You can choose to end your addiction. You can drastically improve the quality of your life—not out of fear for the future, but because you want to make something beautiful of your life right now.

Some time ago, a young woman came to one of my training programs. Doctors had recently detected a tumor in her brain. She had maybe one year left to live. And she wanted to quit smoking. She wanted her last year of life to be free. She wanted to make something good of her remaining time. She understood what it was all about in life, and I felt a deep respect for her. But I also wondered: Does death have to be staring us in the face before we realize how precious our lives are and how beautiful we can make it? I have made a lot of mistakes in my life. I've also made some good decisions. But, the decision that has had the biggest impact on the rest of my life so far, and the one that made me happiest, was kicking my addiction. I wholeheartedly recommend it.

Chapter 22

Letter to the Future

I saw a movie once about a man who knew that his memory would be completely erased in several weeks. He made extensive tape recordings and written accounts of things that he still wanted to know about himself and his life after the memory lapse had happened. The same goes for almost everybody who quits smoking. Within several weeks or months after quitting you will suffer from a severe form of amnesia.

The human memory works selectively: We forget about bad things more quickly than about good things. In general that's a nice characteristic of our memory, but with quitting smoking it's a disadvantage. This disadvantage is reinforced by another characteristic of the human mind: Things that one feels ashamed of or guilty about will be repressed as soon as possible. The result is often that a smoker, who has quit smoking, will have "forgotten" after several weeks or months why it was he ended his addiction. All the bad feelings of being trapped, the shame of a smoker's coughing fit, the guilt towards others and himself, the dizziness with the first cigarette, the disgust when smoking got out of hand for a while, being powerless against the compulsive thoughts about smoking, all this misery will be forgotten in a fairly short amount of time. What will stay is the illusion that an occasional cigarette did taste good once in a while. Mind you, you won't long for a cigarette. You can easily do without. You are still happy to have quit smoking. But there is a big mistake lying in wait, namely the idea that you have proven that you are in control of smoking, and that you will be able to smoke only a few cigarettes a day now. Later, I will get back to this dangerous misconception. Now I want to talk about the fact that this misconception can only come into existence because you will have forgotten how miserable you felt when you decided to quit smoking. The misery will be repressed and that is a normal phenomenon. It's a form of selective amnesia.

Soon you might have this dangerous kind of amnesia. I can't say if it will take a week, a month or a year, but it is very possible that you will fall for the misconception of being able to stay in control of smoking and allow yourself to have an occasional cigarette. You can give yourself some support now for that possible future situation by carrying out the following instructions. Write a letter to yourself in the future, the time when you will be totally freed from smoking and you have totally forgotten why you wanted to quit smoking so badly. Write a nice letter, with a proper beginning. Write the way you would write to your best friend, your lover, or your own child whom you want to save from a serious mistake. Remind this future you about the reasons why you want to quit smoking so badly. Write about the vexations, the coughing fits, the feelings of guilt, and the fears. Write also about how scared you are of quitting, how scary and empty life after quitting looks through the eyes of an addict. Give yourself the best advice you can muster. Give yourself the most loving advice that flows from your heart. Write this letter before reading the rest of this book. Keep the letter in this book. Keep this book in a place that's accessible only to you. The more care you give to this letter now, the easier it will be for you later on to leave this miserable addiction behind you for good.

Chapter 23

The Right Motivation

There are quite a few reasons for wanting to give up smoking. We've discussed most of them in previous chapters. Still it might be a good idea to list all the reasons one could have for quitting smoking. Believe it or not, there are some improper reasons to quit! If you quit with one of those improper reasons in the back of your head, there is a risk of failure. In this chapter, you can check your motivation.

We know very well by now that every smoker is afraid to quit smoking. As in the saying, "to set a thief to catch a thief," some people will try to fight this fear with another fear. That could be the fear of a terrible disease caused by smoking or the fear of losing your job because your boss is very strongly opposed to smoking or the fear of losing your partner because he thinks you stink. We already named the fear of losing face if your attempt to quit is a failure.

All these fears might seem to support you with quitting, but actually they work against you. For they obscure the real reason to quit, namely, that it is a wonderful feeling not to be addicted anymore. If you quit for fear of something else, you will maintain the idea that smoking in itself was nice, but that you can't do it anymore for fear of that other thing.

The fear that every smoker feels before quitting is very normal. That fear will make you unbelievably relieved if you finally make the decision that scares you so much. The fear of quitting will become your best friend after quitting. Don't try to hide this fear behind other fears. Quitting smoking is not something you do out of fear for negative consequences in the future, but out of a desire for immediate positive consequences. It is out of desire for freedom, health, and high self-esteem.

Another reason to quit smoking might be the amount of money that it will save you. The average smoker spends around two thousand dollars a year on cigarettes. It's amusing to calculate how much money you would spend on smoking if you don't quit and if you live to the age of seventy. For me, that would be twenty-five thousand dollars! That's about the same amount of money that I have already spent in the twenty-five years that I smoked.

A fairly heavy smoker can easily smoke away seventy-five thousand dollars in a lifetime or more! What a great reason to quit, right?

Well, it's not. I don't know about you, but I always threw one pack of cigarettes in my basket at the supermarket and paid for it together with all my other groceries. Nowadays, I don't throw this pack of cigarettes in the basket, but at the end of the month my money is still finished. By the way, did you ever wonder why such a small number of smokers buy a carton of cigarettes at a time? If you need a stick of butter every day, you would always buy twelve or twenty-four at a time, wouldn't you? You would also never buy just one egg a day. Still, very few cartons of cigarettes are sold. There is only one reason: Smokers are ashamed of paying forty dollars at a time for something that they actually want to get rid of. They would much rather conceal one or two packs in their groceries every day. You don't quit smoking to save money.

Of course, it's so much for the better that you will save thousands of dollars a year for the rest of your life. But you won't be able to tell much by your bank account. Money has the strange tendency to run out, at least with me it has, no matter what I do. I also have to warn you about the notion of the "savings fund." Some people set aside the money that they would otherwise have spent on cigarettes. They promise themselves that they can spend this money on a nice long weekend as a reward for not smoking for three months. What do you mean, a reward! To be freed from this lousy addiction, that's the reward for quitting! With every notion of a reward, you will reinforce the idea that it is a punishment not to smoke anymore. That's an idea that belongs to the addiction, however. In that way, you sneak in through the back door what you got rid of through the front door when you quit. So watch out for reward systems.

Has someone promised you a trip when you "keep it up" for a year? What do you mean, keep it up? It's great to be freed from smoking. You even will be surprised that you kept up smoking for such a long time! You quit because you want to, not to earn a trip. Of course, everybody is free to offer you a trip after a year, but only when they want to do so, out of admiration for you.

Did you make a bet? Triple wrong: The reward, the loss of money with failure and the fear of losing face will all work against you. Every reward will work counter-productively. Quitting smoking has only one goal: To be freed from that oppressing addiction. There is only one reward, and you will get it from the first day after you quit. The reward is relief, independence, pride, energy, vitality, health, and a big surge in self-respect.

A special case of improper motivation might occur when you try quitting together with somebody else. Sometimes if you quit together with a friend or colleague, a rivalry arises, a kind of competition of who will keep up the longest. The fear of losing face could play a role in this situation, so that the quitting will be in danger. But if there is no rivalry at all, like with intimate friends, or lovers, some motivational problems could occur as well. That was the case with an older couple, in which the man was told to quit by his doctor because he suffered from some serious health problems. He attended the *Free Will Training* program and was happy to be freed from smoking. His wife stopped smoking with him. She was more concerned about his health than about her own. After several days, she called to say that she was going crazy with craving. She felt extra guilty about her craving, because she felt she was breaking solidarity with her husband. She was very scared to start smoking again, because she was afraid that he would start again if she did.

I have had couples in my training program before, and sometimes it can work very well to quit together with your beloved. You can tell each other about how relieved you are and sometimes about the difficult moments that you have. But it is extremely important to be clear on the fact that each person quits for himself. No solidarity, no supporting one another in difficult times. There is only one reason to quit smoking: to be free of addiction. If you quit together with your partner you should give each other total permission to succeed or fail. Don't be afraid that it will be harder for you if your partner starts smoking again. If you quit in the right way (more about that later in this book), it won't make any difference at all. You will feel compassion for your partner because he doesn't feel the happiness you feel after escaping from the addiction. On the other hand, your partner might get inspired by your success and quit later on anyway. Let each other be free. Be responsible only for your own results and tell each other everything you feel, including that you don't believe quitting will work at all. If you keep all this in mind, quitting smoking together can become a delightful experience. Shared joy is doubled joy!

Finally, there is a kind of improper motivation that has to do with the relationship you have with yourself. Some people prepare for quitting by making a solemn promise to themselves, by making a very tough deal with themselves, or by being hard on themselves in another way. This looks like making a bet with friends, but now it is a bet with yourself. Now too, you are deriving your motivation from fear of losing face, but instad it's losing face with yourself. You boost yourself with intentions, deals with yourself, threats to yourself, rewards for yourself, and it throws you from the frying pan into the fire. Quitting smoking is not something you can do by force. You can't end an addiction by putting yourself under pressure. The decision to definitely step out of your addiction can only spring from gentleness, from care for yourself, from love for yourself and for life. As long as you can hold on to that feeling, and to the realization that you only want the best for yourself, you will never long for a cigarette anymore. Then you will truly never have to smoke anymore.

Chapter 24

Reasons to Keep Smoking

After a chapter about motivations to quit smoking, we should have one about reasons to keep smoking. In previous chapters, all fallacies that smokers come up with for their dependency on nicotine have passed revue already. You cannot tell yourself any longer now that smoking helps you to concentrate better, nor that it chases away boredom. It's also impossible to hold any longer that it helps you to cope with stress, or that it fosters relaxation. The fact that smoking still tastes good once in a while (aside from all those cigarettes that disgust you) is a consequence of the addiction, not a cause for it. As soon as you step out of the addiction, you won't think smoking tastes good anymore. You will long for a cigarette as much as you will long for hitting your big toe with a hammer.

A subtler reason is the seeming advantage of smoking as a means to control your mood changes. Every cigarette dissolves part of your bad feelings (by compensating for withdrawal); bad feelings by the way, that were only caused by the previous cigarette. We have seen earlier in this book that such an improvement of your mood will in the long run make you more powerless regarding your feelings. Each time you need a cigarette to improve your mood (to make it less bad), you reinforce the feeling that you don't have any influence on the way you feel. And you enhance your dependence on smoking.

Still, it is important to make a clear choice. Smoking is a means to cover up insecurity in some situations. The options include: choosing to cover up your insecurity (by which you will only enlarge it), or choosing to accept your insecurity as a normal human characteristic (by which your insecurity will become lessened). There are several choices like this. Do you choose to subdue your stress with a cigarette (by which the stress will become worse in the end), or do you choose to accept this stress as a normal, human phenomenon that can help you perform your task (by which the stress will diminish)?

All these choices can be traced back to a fundamental choice between two possibilities. The first one is maintaining a facade of illusions, such as the illusion of adulthood, of self-confidence, or of support in difficult times. Behind this facade you keep feeling puny, dependent and insecure. The second possibility is the choice to quit smoking, the choice to shatter the illusion, the choice for true independence, confidence and self-esteem.

It's important not to approach this decision hastily. Before you can definitely leave your smoke addiction behind, you must be sure that there is absolutely nothing valuable in it for you. I suggest that you reflect on your reasons for smoking for the next few minutes. Check to see if perhaps you can still find a reason to smoke without feeling confined and unhealthy. Do you still believe that it's possible to stay in control of smoking if you smoke just one cigarette once in a while? Do you think, somewhere in the back of your head, that it could be possible to enjoy a cigarette without feeling guilty about it? Keep smoking then! Keep smoking and start right away with enjoying every cigarette. Start right away with only smoking those cigarettes that you light out of your own free will. Do it now, instead of hoping to become a healthy and happy smoker in the future.

I warn you, it is ten times more difficult to smoke less and "consciously" than to quit totally and forever. For in the first case, you'll still be a smoker, who has to control himself all the time and who has to fight against the compulsive thoughts about cigarettes. In the second case, you will no longer be addicted, and there will be no need for a cigarette.

Is there absolutely no way to maintain smoking without suffering the disadvantages of being addicted? Think thoroughly about it. You have been addicted for such a long time, so don't give up too easily now. For you don't want to quit for a week or a year, but you want to get rid of all the addiction troubles for good. It's normal that you still feel fear. But if you're still in doubt as to whether you really want to quit, take some more time to think about it. When you've finished this chapter, put this book down for a moment. Make yourself a drink and smoke a cigarette. Try to enjoy it as consciously as possible. Does it taste good? Then wonder over this strange and absurd addiction that makes something filthy taste good and that makes you long for something that destroys you. Does it taste bad? Then rejoice in the fact that soon you will never have to smoke again.

Chapter 25

Why Other Methods Don't Work and the Free Yourself Method Does

Most methods, which are designed to make quitting smoking easier, focus on repressing the physical withdrawal. But this physical withdrawal amounts to so little! It's the psychological addiction that needs to be surmounted. It is despite these methods, and not thanks to them, that some people still succeed in quitting. Let's take a closer look at some of these methods.

There are nicotine patches and chewing gum. These make sure that the nicotine level in your blood stays the same without smoking any cigarettes. In fact, you still suffer the difficulties of quitting (i.e. not smoking anymore), while the nicotine addiction is being maintained. The idea, of course, is to gradually use fewer and fewer patches or less chewing gum, so that you won't need nicotine anymore after some time. In fact, you just prolong the addiction.

Besides, nicotine patches and chewing gum suggest that this physical withdrawal is very hard to conquer. And behind that is the conviction that smoking really is an enjoyable thing to do and that it is terribly hard to quit. But it is not! The physical withdrawal doesn't amount to anything much (I will get back to this later). It's these deep-rooted misconceptions about the effect of nicotine, this ineradicable illusion about the good taste of smoking, that makes the addiction so obstinate.

There are other methods designed to repress the physical withdrawal symptoms, such as acupuncture and laser treatment. Again, these methods repress the least difficult part of overcoming a smoking addiction- Besides, they strengthen the misconceptions that make an addicted person keep smoking. Even if you succeed in quitting with one of these methods, you will always miss the smoking in the back of your mind. You will keep thinking that a cigarette did taste good once in a while. And on a bad day, when the difficulties are too much for you, you will fall back to your addiction, which you never completely escaped in the first place. The same is valid for Zyban or Wellbutrin, which are antidepressants, that help to repress the difficulties after quitting the wrong way.

Methods based on hypnosis go a bit further than addressing only the physical side of the addiction. Certain psychological aspects of the addiction, like compulsive thinking about smoking, can be temporarily repressed. Nevertheless, this method is insufficient too, because it doesn't break the most essential illusions of the addiction: That smoking (sometimes) tastes really good, that it can be a big help in difficult moments, and that it's extremely hard not to do it anymore after quitting. Here we find one of the most important differences between the Free Yourself Method and most other methods. The other methods suggest that the hard part of quitting smoking starts after you quit, namely the battle against the longing. The Free Yourself Method turns this concept around: The hard part of quitting is making a definite decision. After that, it is a piece of cake—no torment and misery, but relief and happiness.

It is actually easy to explain this difference. Addiction is synonymous to dependence and powerlessness. With other quitting methods, this powerlessness is only being deepened. For these methods suggest that you are too weak to quit by yourself, that you need a trick, a device to help you. These methods strengthen the fear that every addicted person already feels very strongly, that it will be terribly difficult never to touch a cigarette again. These methods (partially) maintain the addiction. Maybe some people will succeed in quitting smoking in this way, but they will always, psychologically, hold on to part of their addiction and all the risks that are involved.

There is only one way to quit smoking definitely and without withdrawal misery: To independently, without using any tricks or devices, very consciously *decide* never to smoke again. The funny thing is, that after making this decision, your addiction will explode like a pricked balloon, and it will become apparent that it's not a problem at all not to smoke anymore. The other methods are methods based on fear, and they provide for that which the addicted fears—a hard struggle that can never be totally won. The Free Yourself Method is the method of independence and the desire for freedom and purity. This method gives what every smoker longs for the most—the immediate ending of the struggle with himself, the end of the addiction misery and the beginning of a new life, in which smoking doesn't play any part. The only disadvantage of this method is that you will have to do it all by yourself. And that is, at the same time, the greatest advantage! Nobody and nothing can take away from you what you have accomplished on your own. It becomes a part of your. It gives you a new feeling of self-esteem, and that means the irrevocable end of your smoking addiction.

Chapter 26

Practical Guidelines for After Quitting

The first days after quitting smoking, I felt mostly very festive. Of course, I thought about smoking a lot, but the absence of any compulsion and the realization that I wasn't forced anymore gave me an incredible feeling of liberation and relief. Certainly, you feel the physical withdrawal symptoms once in a while, like a light ticklish and hollow feeling in the stomach. But then, it feels as if a big cleanup is underway. I imagined a lot of mops and scrubbers at work inside of me, removing the residues of nicotine from my body. You can support this cleanup by eating a lot of fruit during the first days and by planning some extra exercise. A long walk or bicycle ride will surely enhance the festive feeling of the first days. For a cleanup, a lot of water is needed. Drink a glass of water every time you feel this hollow feeling.

These physical "clean-up symptoms" usually last three to five days. For some it can take a little longer, but never longer than three weeks. After three weeks, it is absolutely impossible to have any physical reaction due to quitting smoking. Difficult moments, if they are there at all, are without exception of a mental nature. In the next chapters, you will find a lot of guidelines for preventing these difficult moments and—when you still have one anyway—how to react in such a way that they pass in a few minutes. But let me get this straight: These difficult moments don't look at all like the difficulties that a smoker fears when he thinks of quitting. During the few difficult moments I had after quitting, there wasn't a second that I felt like starting to smoke again. Difficult moments are moments in which it seems, for a short period of time, that you miss smoking. They are illusions, remains from an addicted past that don't suit you at all anymore. But they can make you very cranky anyway if you react to them in the wrong way.

The next chapters can be seen as direction signs in the new country of independence. For although you are freed from smoking from the first day on, you are so used to not being free, that sometimes you will create difficulties where there aren't any. In the same way that the smoke addiction is like a balloon that you prick at the moment you decide to quit, you can still encounter some little air bubbles in the first weeks and months after quitting. If you are not prepared for these phenomena, the danger exists that you will blow up these little balloons, so that you will get yourself into some serious trouble. As soon as you recognize these little balloons however, you will be able to prick them immediately.

Quitting smoking actually consists of two parts: the quitting and the not starting again. The Free Yourself Method focuses on both. The way you quit is very important for the period after quitting. It depends on the way you quit, whether the first weeks are weeks of liberation, or weeks of torment and battles with yourself. After that time it is still important to see the traps that can make you fall back into the old addiction. That's what the next chapters are about as well. For sometimes it happens that people start smoking again without even longing for a cigarette at all. Sometimes, people will light a cigarette at the moment that they realize they are no longer addicted.

Addiction is a weird kink in the human mind, and in the next chapters, you can find out everything about it. If you read them carefully, nothing unexpected will happen to you. You will be able to reduce the difficult moments to a minimum and your freedom won't be in danger at all. Before the moment of quitting, you will already know the whole road that comes after it, and you will have mapped out your route. The next chapters will be a preparation for the nicest holiday you will ever plan, a holiday that will take the rest of your life, a holiday in which you will feel clean and honest with yourself.

Chapter 27

The Fear of Thoughts

A lot of smokers are scared that they will keep thinking of smoking all the time after quitting. So on the first day after quitting, they try to ban every thought about smoking from their minds. In doing that, they make the biggest mistake that an ex-smoker can make. As soon as you try to repress a thought, you give power to that thought. By pushing away the thought of a cigarette, you will make that thought into an obsession within several hours. It will seem as if there is only one way of getting rid of this miserable thought of a cigarette—by lighting one. The attempt to quit will fail within a few hours or days. The cause: fear of a thought.

In psychology, some experiments have been done with the pushing away of thoughts. One of these experiments went like this: A group of people got the assignment not to think of a white bear for five minutes. After that, they had to think of a white bear for five minutes. Another group got the reverse assignment: First think of a white bear for five minutes and then not think of the white bear. The results of the experiment were remarkable; nobody could not think of a white bear for five minutes. Besides, there was a lot more thinking of the animal in the period that it wasn't allowed than in the period that it was obligatory. Trying not to have a thought will cause this thought to return more often and to become stronger.

With thinking of a white bear, feelings are neutral. In some cases, a thought is accompanied by fear. A mild case of this is well known to a lot of people. Lying in bed, you suddenly think: Did I lock the front door tonight? You push this thought aside, because you don't feel like getting up. The thought returns a little stronger, fueled by a slightly unsafe feeling. Although you are actually almost sure that you did lock the door, by pushing away the thought of it, it becomes a compulsive thought and within five minutes you will get out of bed to check the front door—which will be locked, indeed, as you expected.

As a smoker, you push away the thought of smoking dozens of times a day. If you did smoke a cigarette every time you thought about it, you would maybe smoke five packs a day. By pushing away the thought of a cigarette, you make this thought into an obsession very quickly. Thereupon, you want to get rid of this annoying thought of smoking, and the longing for a cigarette will become stronger and stronger. At last, you light a cigarette and for a short time, you are freed from that compulsive thought of smoking. After extinguishing the cigarette, the cycle starts anew: thinking of a cigarette, pushing away the thought, creating a compulsive thought, longing to be freed from the obsession, lighting another cigarette. At the same time, the smoker becomes increasingly worried about not being able to get rid of the obsession anymore. Imagine suffering from compulsive thoughts for the rest of your life without being able to escape this for a moment by lighting a cigarette! But don't panic: This fear belongs to your addiction. It is a consequence of your addiction and will disappear the moment you kick the habit. It's the smoker who suffers from compulsive thoughts, not the ex-smoker.

When you quit smoking, for the first days and weeks you will think a lot about smoking. There is no reason to be afraid of that, because with every thought of cigarettes, you will feel that you don't have to light one anymore. Every thought of cigarettes will give you a sense of freedom, of independence, of being in control of what you do and what you don't do. The biggest mistake you can make is pushing away thoughts about smoking. It is absolutely normal that you think a lot of smoking after quitting. By accepting this as a normal fact, by even enjoying thinking about smoking and the feeling of freedom that comes with it, your thoughts about smoking will gradually disappear. More and more often, you will discover that you have not been thinking of smoking for a whole hour, or for several hours. By all means, don't be irritated by your thoughts of smoking. Did you think you could quit having thoughts that you had for years, dozens of times a day, just like that? It's normal for an ex-smoker to think about smoking dozens of times a day for the first weeks and months. Those thoughts don't mean anything anymore. They are no longer accompanied by feelings of powerlessness and frustration about not being able to keep yourself free from this filthy addiction. What you will feel with every thought of smoking will be independence, freedom and relief. And every day you will think a little less of smoking than the previous day. On the one hand, that is a pity: after a while it is so normal not to smoke anymore. Still, also after months and years of not smoking, you will sometimes get the happy feeling that you got rid of it for good.

Chapter 28

There Is No Such Thing As One Cigarette

A very big misconception about quitting smoking is the thought that there is such a thing as "just one." With addictions there is only one law: Either you are addicted or you aren't. When you are not, you don't need a cigarette. The situations in which the ex-smoker thinks that it can't hurt to light just one will be treated extensively later on. The thought "just one" arises at a difficult moment, when you have been pushing away the thought of a cigarette. This thought will become stronger because of that. But you don't want to decide to start smoking again. On the other hand, the idea of never smoking again is too heavy for you at the moment. The way out seems to be to smoke "just one." This is a fool's way out, and that's why it means a relapse in the addiction. For an addict doesn't really decide anything—to quit or to keep smoking. An addict simply fools with himself.

"Just one, to prove that I don't like it anymore." Of course there is a big chance that this cigarette will taste filthy, after days or weeks of not smoking. So you will say, pleased, "See, I really got rid of it." Meanwhile, the nicotine of this one cigarette starts building a light withdrawal in your body again. Within a few days, you will think again that "just one" does no harm. And slowly, without having to really decide, you will start smoking again. Let it sink in for once and for all:

THERE IS NO SUCH THING
AS ONE CIGARETTE!

One cigarette is the start of the chain of withdrawal that you have to neutralize with the next cigarette, that will cause withdrawal again, that you will have to neutralize with the next cigarette, and so on. Smoking one cigarette never proves that you got rid of it; it proves that you are starting again. Of course, for the first weeks or months, you will smoke less, and for a while, you will feel that you are pretty much in control. But there is no such thing as smoking without addiction, nor addiction without dependence, nor dependence without confinement and self-hatred. Within a short period of time, you will have to start quitting all over again. No addiction exists without the wish not to be addicted.

Chapter 29

Smoking Is Always Allowed

One of the biggest mistakes you can make after quitting is telling yourself that you are never allowed to smoke anymore. Psychologically, that will have the effect of the red flag on the bull. The effect will be an enlargement of the results that came out of the experiment of not being allowed to think of a white bear. Not being allowed to think something will enhance this thought. If you forbid yourself to ever smoke again, you strengthen the misconception that smoking is desirable. That's why a total ban on smoking in our society, or even a prohibition of selling tobacco, would have a totally opposite effect. A lot of people, especially the youth, would feel a lot more attracted to smoking.

Usually, the idea that you are not allowed to smoke comes into being as follows. There is a difficult moment, because of a certain event or situation. Later on in this book, I will talk more about these difficult situations. In this difficult situation, the thought of a cigarette arises. You make your first mistake and push this thought aside. Thus, this thought becomes stronger, and after awhile it has become compulsive, an obsession. You long for the end of this obsession, so you long for a cigarette. You don't want to start smoking again, though. For a second, you think, "Just one." But well, you have read the Free Yourself Method book, so you know that smoking one cigarette equals starting smoking again. So you tell yourself, "No, I'm not allowed to smoke again." You threaten yourself with hell and damnation if you take a cigarette. You forbid yourself. In fact, you are starting a willpower fight with yourself. You can never win this fight. The only thing you can do is try not to lose for some time, but a miserable time that will be. And all this is only because you pushed aside the thought of a cigarette, and because you forbade yourself to smoke. What do you mean, "I'm not allowed to smoke anymore?" Of course, you can smoke. There is no law that forbids smoking. You are absolutely free to smoke whenever you want to. It's the smoke addict who is not free, who feels the urge to do something that he actually doesn't want to do. It is the smoke addict who tells himself, "I actually shouldn't smoke," and who feels guilty about doing it. You quit smoking in order to feel free, and then you put yourself in another jail immediately—the jail of "I'm not allowed to smoke ever again." Never tell yourself that you are not allowed to smoke anymore. For only if you feel that you are allowed to smoke, you can choose not to. Not being allowed to smoke is one of the most vicious twists in the mind of the addict. For how long have you been smoking and for how long have you been wishing to be freed from your addiction? For how long already are you longing for purity and independence? And then, after a long and heavy fight with your fears, you have taken the difficult decision to step out of the addiction, to choose for yourself, your health and your freedom. What do you mean, "I'm not allowed to smoke anymore?" Replace the word "smoking" with the synonymous "being addicted," and look what you are saying, "I'm not allowed to be addicted." Do you see what nonsense that is?

Maybe you will have some difficult moments after you quit. The only thing that you need to do at such a moment is to realize that this is only a short after-effect of your former addiction. Don't do anything more! Don't push away the thought of a cigarette! Never say, "I'm not allowed to smoke." Every human being is absolutely free to destroy himself in the way that he chooses. The question is: Do you really want that? Or would you rather be good to yourself? If ever you get a difficult moment, then think back to why you decided to quit smoking. And don't do anything else at all!!! The bad feeling will pass in a few minutes.

Chapter 30

Avoidance

You have already understood from the previous chapters that fear is a bad adviser with quitting smoking. You push away the thought of smoking because you are afraid that thinking about it will make you long for it. This pushing away creates the obsession and the longing. You tell yourself that you are not allowed to smoke, because you are afraid that you will take another cigarette. By doing this, you make smoking into something attractive, and you forget why it was that you wanted to quit so badly. It is not the thought of smoking or even the longing for a cigarette that makes you slide back into the addiction. It's the fear of the thought of smoking and the fear of longing for a cigarette that give the addiction a chance again. In fact, nothing can go wrong as long as you remember what it's like to be addicted, and as long as you realize how good it feels to grant yourself a life without addiction.

Fear is telling us that it's better to avoid certain situations after quitting smoking, the kind of situations that we think are going to be hard. But avoiding these situations equals pushing away the thought of a cigarette. By avoiding certain situations out of fear for a difficult moment, you empower that fear and you limit your freedom, thus creating the difficulties that you were afraid of. Sooner or later, you will get into these situations anyway, so why wait?

Maybe you have a good friend who is a "dedicated" smoker. Somebody who is not capable of acknowledging to himself and others that he is addicted. You will maybe feel inclined not to hang out with this friend for a while. In that case, search your motives thoroughly. Was your friendship maybe based on your shared addiction? In that case, the need to see each other will decrease sure enough. But if you avoid seeing him out of fear for wanting a cigarette, then go see this friend as soon as possible. Realize that your friend will envy you, instead of the other way around. A real friend will be happy for you, will give you compliments, and will not in any way try to persuade you to smoke a cigarette.

The previous example applies to all sorts of social events in which people smoke. Campfire at the beach, having dinner with friends who smoke, going to a party, don't avoid it! The same goes for all situations in which you used to smoke a lot. If it is a stressful meeting with your boss do then it right away. If it is a long car trip, take some favorite music with you and go. If it is a difficult job that needs a lot of concentration, then you will notice that it's even easier without smoking. Each time that you postpone these things or try to avoid them, you are letting fear rule and you only enlarge the problems that you were trying to avoid. Each time that you walk into these situations with open eyes, you will feel your own power, and you will enhance your independence and your self-esteem. And even if it would happen that you have a difficult moment in one of these situations, it is always better to experience this right after quitting than a lot later. For when you've just quit, it's easier to accept the fact that you are having a difficult moment. But having a difficult moment months after quitting will make you a lot crankier. I will give you an example.

I'm a sailor. I often go away in my old wooden two-master for a week or so during the summer. Sailing can be quite exciting, but it can also be pretty boring, and one always does it with others on a big boat like that. These are all situations in which a smoker smokes more than usual. I quit smoking in autumn, right after the closing of the sailing season. The first time I went sailing as a non-smoker was more than six months later. It had already been months since I'd had my last difficult moment.

But the sails were only just hoisted, someone brought the coffee up on deck, and I couldn't stop thinking of smoking. For me, smoking was still attached to sailing, because this was my first time as a non-smoker. By the way, I didn't really feel inclined to smoke. For I'm much too happy that I got rid of it. But the thought of smoking made me irritable those first days of sailing. I didn't think those thoughts still suited me. After some lovely sailing days, however, those thoughts disappeared by themselves, and I became a happy non-smoking sailor.

As an ex-smoker, you feel the strongest during the first days and weeks after quitting. The feeling that you don't need to smoke anymore is still new. You are so happy about the air that you breathe. You feel your condition is getting better every day. Your new independence will give you strong self-esteem. You should take advantage of this new power by diving into all situations that scare you. You will hit two birds with one stone, because every time you conquer a difficult situation (and that will appear to be much easier than you thought), you will deepen your sense of independence and increase your self-esteem.

Thus, you will turn quitting into a vehicle that can change your life in other areas. I have met quitters who've asked for a performance review from their boss right away, quitters who have confronted a colleague who they were having a hard time with, and quitters who finally dared to ask their nice neighbor to go out for a cup of coffee.

As weak as you feel while you are addicted, so strong you will feel during the time after quitting. It depends on you whether you will use that force for other things as well—if you will go further down the path of independence and freedom. You got rid of smoking already.

Why is it that quitting smoking gives us so much new power and inspiration? All these positive feelings are the result of keeping to a decision that scared you so much: definitely quitting smoking. You wanted to quit and you were also scared of it. When you long for something that also scares you, it gives an enormous amount of strength and self-esteem when you no longer avoid your fear. Conquering fear doesn't mean not feeling that fear anymore. It means to accept fear for what it is, and to strive for the goal of taking your fear along with you. That's why it is so good right after quitting to go and look for all the situations that might still scare you, those situations in which you think it might be hard not to smoke.

And that's why it works so well not to avoid all other situations in your life that scare you. Sometimes they're small things. I used to behave a lot more scared than I do now. When somebody in a store arrogantly and obviously doesn't wait for his turn, I dare to say in a friendly but firm manner that it's my turn now. It still makes me feel strong. Everybody has private desires that are clothed in fear. Would you like to tell your parents how you have experienced your youth with them? Are some things in your relationship not going too well, but are you too afraid to confront them? Would you like to give a bunch of flowers to somebody you like, just like that, and are you afraid that she will think that's weird? All these things could easily be left alone. That's an option that you probably already know very well. Try something new for a change. Do what you are afraid of. To start, by getting out of this miserable addiction. I can assure you: it is a fantastic experience!

Chapter 31

Proper Planning

Most people that are seriously considering quitting smoking will start seeing a lot of reasons why it is more sensible to wait a little longer. Here is an anthology of the many reasons to postpone quitting.

- I should wait until after my examination, because I'll be calmer then.
- First my best friend's wedding, then I'll quit.
- I will quit right after my vacation, so that I can still enjoy it.
- I will quit right before my vacation, so that I don't need to go to work the first weeks.
- I will quit in summer, because in winter, I'll be too depressed.

- I will quit in winter, because it will be easier to stay at home.
- I will wait to quit until I'm in a relationship again; that makes me calmer.
- I will quit after I break up with my partner, because she smokes like a chimney.
- I will quit when I have the flu again, because I don't enjoy smoking then anyway.
- I will quit when I'm no longer ill, because then I'll be able to start exercising right away.

All reasoning that tells you it's better to postpone quitting for a while longer is in fact an expression of fear. And it's better not to give in to fear, because then you are curtailing your freedom. The best moment to quit is always NOW. Are there no reasons at all, then, to quit at a certain time?

In principal, it doesn't matter at all at what moment you quit. If you quit the day before your examination or the day after, it doesn't matter. As soon as you have quit, you don't have to smoke anymore, never mind if you are in a stressful situation. For why would you make this stress worse by lighting another cigarette? Quitting smoking is a treat, and why would you postpone this treat? Why wait until after your examination? If you don't smoke, it's easier to concentrate. Why wait until after your best friend's wedding? If you don't smoke, it's easier to relax, and you will be able to enjoy yourself without first having to light a cigarette all the time.

The only planning that could make sense is to fix the day and the hour whereupon you will smoke your last cigarette. There are seven days in a week, so it can never take long before your favorite day of the week has come. I myself smoked my last cigarette on a Sunday night around midnight. For me, Mondays always have the feeling of "starting all over," and my first day as a non-smoker had to be a Monday. Besides, it seemed nice to have a good night's sleep after my last cigarette and to wake up the next day as a non-smoker.

But I have heard a lot of stories of the moments other people chose to smoke their last cigarette. A lot of people chose Saturday night, so that they could do a lot of fun things and enjoy their first smoke-free day all Sunday long. For the same reasons, Friday night is popular. Some smokers smoke their last cigarette very early in the morning with a beautiful sunrise. Others decide to smoke their last cigarette right after reading the last page of this book. For some, it was an ordinary workday, and the last cigarette was being smoked in seclusion in the bathroom. It doesn't really make a difference for quitting. But make sure that you can experience this moment fully. At the end of this book, I will tell you more about this special event of smoking your last cigarette. But maybe you already have an idea about the day and the moment that you are going to experience this festive occasion.

Chapter 32

The Company of Other Smokers

When you've just quit smoking, you may feel inclined to avoid the company of other smokers. This fear is an understandable—yet for an ex-smoker totally misplaced—remainder of the addiction. It's unfortunate too, because by avoiding smokers, you withhold from yourself the glorious feeling of having escaped an addiction that they are still in the midst of. If anybody is afraid, it's most likely the smoker, whenever he's confronted with somebody who has quit. Maybe he will cover up his insecurities by sceptical remarks, such as, "I'll talk to you in a month or so." But the honorable smoker will always congratulate you for quitting, and he will tell you that it won't be long before he will be "ready for it too." Well, you know from your own experience all the excuses smokers have to procrastinate quitting, so you give them an understanding and reassuring smile.

Actually, it doesn't matter whether you are in the company of smokers or non-smokers. During a sudden difficult moment, however, the company of smokers could ruin your mood even further. In a difficult moment (which I will discuss below), you feel inclined to push away the thought of smoking. The longing for a cigarette that arises because of this is pushed away even more forcefully. An inner conflict arises. Suddenly everybody around you is smoking. And a strange thing happens.

You notice how these smokers are enjoying their cigarettes. With smiling faces and beaming eyes, they inhale the smoke, and with visible pleasure, they puff it out. You feel suddenly lonely, while they are laughing and talking together. You feel weak, whereas they look happy, strong, successful, and self-assured.

You have fallen in the trap of self-pity. And self-pity is a fine way of thoroughly demolishing your self-esteem. At such a hard moment, pity is the last thing you need. You rather need support and encouragement. Start with admitting that you are having a hard time. Don't resist it; don't make a big deal out of it; everybody has a difficult moment once in a while. Just realize that this difficult moment is the last convulsion of that lousy addiction to smoking. If you don't do anything else, the difficult moment will pass in a few minutes. In the meantime, instead of running away from those seemingly happy smokers, you should study them carefully.

Why do those smokers look so happy when they light a cigarette? It's only logical: The cigarette helps them to stop thinking of smoking for a while. Maybe they were already fighting with themselves for fifteen minutes or half an hour, in order to postpone that next cigarette. Finally they light it, and for one moment, during the first whiffs of that cigarette, they feel freed from their addiction. The second half of the cigarette tastes less good, and the last whiffs are often just filthy, but most smokers are pretty good at not showing that. Only after they've lit the next cigarette are they able to enjoy what's going on around them. Did you think those smokers enjoy their cigarettes? No. They are forced to light a cigarette again and again; otherwise they can't enjoy what's going on at all.

Watch closely when you are having a difficult moment. Imagine how they will feel when they go to bed at the end of the evening with a parched mouth. And how they will feel the next morning, with the taste of a dead mouse in their mouth. You are only having a difficult moment. They are having a difficult addiction. Silently, they are jealous of you and of every non-smoker. You think that you feel insecure in this difficult moment? That's nothing compared to the insecurity and weakness that they experience, as addicts.

The company of smokers is not scary at all anymore for the ex-smoker. One nice thing about quitting with the Free Yourself Method is that you won't turn into a fanatical anti-smoking crusader. Those anti-smokers are often frustrated ex-smokers, who want to fight smoking with all their might. They are often still a little bit addicted in their minds. If you are a successful ex-smoker, however, you will only feel compassion for the addicted smoker. You can help her by telling her how easy it was for you to quit. But leave her alone otherwise. It's already hard enough for her with her constant self-criticism, forced self-mutilation, lack of fresh air, and the stink in her clothes and her skin. Sometimes you will have a difficult moment being an ex-smoker. You don't have to do anything, not even light a cigarette, and it will pass in a few minutes. That's something that makes every smoker jealous.

Chapter 33

Substitutes

The use of any kind of substitute after quitting smoking is superfluous and will increase the risk of falling back into the addiction. That's because by using substitutes you enhance the feeling that you miss smoking. Substitutes are made for—and made by—people who have quit smoking without stepping out of the addiction. There are the nicotine patches and nicotine chewing gum, which were already discussed in chapter 25.

Very common substitutes for cigarettes are the pipe and the cigar. It happens often that someone quits smoking and walks around with a smelly pipe a few weeks later. He doesn't really like it, but it is better than nothing. A need to smoke is being maintained here. For whether you inhale that smoke or not, with every pipe you light, you tell yourself that you'd rather light a cigarette, but that you are "not allowed to do that anymore, because you've quit." Oh, stop fooling yourself! If you really think that that cigarette has something to offer you, that you can enjoy it without feeling guilty, then light it right away. Don't torture yourself with a pipe, in which the tobacco juice mixes with your saliva, burning all your taste buds. Don't torture yourself with a cigar, the smoke of which smells ten times worse than a cigarette's. Don't torture yourself with a substitute that maintains the illusion that a cigarette tastes a lot nicer. The same goes for cigarettes without nicotine, sometimes called "herbal cigarettes." For the smoking addict, they are the same as alcohol-free beer for the alcoholic. Or seawater for the shipwrecked—if you drink it you will get thirstier. Don't torture yourself with these fake solutions. It is a treat not to have to smoke anymore. Don't spoil this treat with these substitutes for smoking. If you quit smoking using the Free Yourself Method, you will usually start drinking less alcohol too. For a great deal of the beer, wine, or distilled liquor that you drank only served the purpose of compensating for the horrible taste of smoking. Especially at parties or in a bar, where you usually smoke more than average, your throat gets overburdened by smoking. A drink moistens the throat again and helps you stand the next cigarettes better. As a non-smoker, you will also drink once in a while. But only for the taste of it and for the effect of the drinking itself.

If you notice that you start drinking more after quitting smoking, this means that you are using alcohol as a substitute for smoking. You are trying to repress the insecurity that you used to hide with a cigarette—with alcohol now. Be attentive to this development and ask yourself if you want to swap one addiction for another. It's better to focus on "missing the cigarette" and wonder why you keep holding on to that illusion. Did you issue a prohibition on smoking without realizing? Did you unconsciously tell yourself that you weren't allowed to smoke anymore? Then stop that. Of course you can smoke. Nobody denies you the right to destroy yourself. But is that what you truly want? And while you're at it, also check which alcoholic beverages you drink because you like them and which ones you imbibe out of a need to escape, or just because you can't refrain from it. Be honest with yourself. How is your life supposed to become really happy if you keep fooling yourself all the time?

There are countless other substitutes that seem to be very innocent in themselves. About snacks and food, an extra chapter is coming up. There is also a chapter about soft drugs and other drugs. In principle, any action or occupation can degenerate into a substitute for smoking. Do you suddenly watch a lot more television after quitting smoking? Do you play the same computer game for hours at a time? Do you go jogging five times a day? Do you dig up your garden three times a week and vacuum the house three times a day? In all these cases, you are probably filling up the missing of smoking. You keep running around and doing all kinds of things, in order to try not to think of smoking. Sure enough, substitutes are often disguised ways of pushing away the thought of smoking. And as you know, this pushing away works backwards. As a smoke addict you were running away all the time from the thought of quitting and your own responsibility. If you keep running away from yourself and your own thoughts after quitting, you are welcoming your addiction in through the back door. As soon as you notice yourself running away from the thought of smoking, have a serious talk with yourself. Don't kick yourself, but be understanding of your behavior. Ask yourself if you are going to achieve your goal in this way. Ask yourself if you would rather be addicted again. Then make the free choice of not being addicted again. You will notice that such a heart-to-heart talk with yourself can be a true relief.

Chapter 34

Soft and Other Drugs

If you are used to regularly smoking a joint (marihuana, hashish and the like), you'll have a small extra problem when you quit smoking. Of course, you will never take a puff of a joint anymore that has tobacco in it. Even one puff of a joint, which has even the slightest amount of tobacco in it, will bring an amount of nicotine in your blood that has to be removed again. This removal will give you withdrawal symptoms. However small and inconspicuous they might be, these symptoms will start up the whole psychological addiction machine again. A day or a week after smoking this joint, you will suddenly feel a light need for a cigarette, also when you haven't smoked for years anymore. I have experienced this myself. I have quit smoking twice before, and both times I didn't smoke for about two years. Two times I started smoking again, because I thought that I had proved to myself that I was in control of smoking. Both times I had coincidentally taken some puffs of a joint a few days earlier, just for fun, because I don't really enjoy the feeling of being stoned anymore. Only years later, I saw the connection between those few puffs of a joint and this vague but unmistakable longing for an "occasional" cigarette.

Although nicotine forms the physical basis for the smoke addiction, after years of smoking there are many more elements to the addiction. For instance, you also get addicted to the prickle of smoke in your throat. That's why it is also not a good idea to smoke joints that consist of only marijuana (without nicotine) after quitting smoking. The prickling of your throat with smoke is such a basic component of the nicotine addiction that it can't occur separately from it. Each nicotine-free joint that you smoke (and the same goes for the nicotine-free "herbal cigarette"), will set the whole psychological addiction machine in motion. You will notice that you smoke more and more joints, as a substitute for the cigarettes that you naturally keep missing anyway. In fact, you remain a smoke addict, but one that is permanently stoned in the long run. Nobody can keep that up. So in the end, you will start smoking cigarettes again.

Actually, there is only one rule that solves this problem: TO QUIT SMOKING, STOP INHALING SMOKE. Whatever it is that you smoke. If being stoned is really that important to you, eat brownies.

I will end this chapter with some words for those people who have another addiction besides smoking, be it alcohol or hard drugs. For your second addiction, the same principles are valid as for the smoke addiction: You can quit from one day to the next, without any withdrawal that is worth mentioning. With heroin and some narcotics, you can get some troublesome side effects. Consult your doctor when you decide to quit. With amphetamines, cocaine, and ecstasy, quitting doesn't result in any physical withdrawal.

Of course, it is possible that this second addiction has seriously dislocated your life. It won't suffice to only get out of your addiction. You may also have to build up your life again. You need help for that. Allow yourself to get that help.

Do you belong to that large group of addicts (either narcotics or uppers, to cocaine or ecstasy) that keeps functioning reasonably well in social and public scenes? Then you can step out of that addiction in one day. The best thing to do is to dump both addictions on the same day. Does this sound too scary to you? Then choose to end the second addiction first. Wait for one or two weeks, until you notice how easy it actually is. Then stop the smoke addiction right away. Use the power that you get from quitting one addiction for ending the other one. By the way, you shouldn't think that it's harder to end two addictions at the same time or shortly after one another. It is a lot more difficult to end one addiction, while leaving the other one intact. Actually, we're not talking about quitting smoking, quitting cocaine, amphetamines, or ecstasy. It's about only one thing: Quitting being addicted. Quit destroying yourself in a hidden and compulsive way. Make a new beginning! Choose freedom and independence! When you are stuck in two addictions, the fear for that choice is naturally twice as big. But if you make this choice anyway, your relief and joy about the regained freedom will be twice as great, too. Don't you feel that it's about time to have some undiluted happiness in your life? Then take that step! And enjoy it.

Chapter 35

The Difficult Moment

During the first months after quitting smoking, you may experience a difficult moment once in a while. A difficult moment is exactly what it says—a very short period of maybe ten or twenty seconds, in which you are having trouble with not smoking anymore. If you don't react properly to such a difficult moment, it can grow into a difficult evening. If you don't react properly to a difficult evening, you can get into serious smoke trouble. The old addiction will reappear, which is usually followed by cigarettes again. That's why this is a very important chapter. For if you react in the right way to a difficult moment, it will be over in a few seconds, after which you will feel even happier that you never have to smoke anymore.

In a difficult moment, you suddenly feel very strongly like smoking. It is a heavy, physical experience, as if your body suddenly really needs a cigarette. Still, it's completely a psychological phenomenon, because your body is already free of nicotine. We call this psychological phenomenon that is disguised as a physical one a "withdrawal pang." When you experience such a withdrawal pang unprepared, it can scare you and make you doubt yourself. You will fear that you won't succeed in quitting, or that you will miss smoking for the rest of your life. You will get angry with yourself and feel you're a weakling. And thus you start up the addiction machine again, for all these thoughts and feelings belong to the old addiction. But if you know what a withdrawal pang is, you are able to see it as a last convulsion of an addicted past. And your problems will be over in mere seconds.

In order to explain what a withdrawal pang is exactly, I have to give you an example of a comparable phenomenon. I will take you back to my own childhood. I lived in the countryside, and since I was seven, I had a friend named Walter. He lived on a big farm, as an only child, with his parents and two live-in uncles. I went to see him every day. We played in the hayloft together; we roamed through the fields and the orchards; we climbed willows or helped out at the farm. I learned how to milk cows there, how to drive a carriage, and how to help cows and sheep giving birth. Today, those skills are fairly useless to me, but I carry them with me as precious memories. The friendship with Walter has always remained, although sometimes we don't see each other for years. He has become some kind of "world farmer:" as a doctor of plant diseases, he travels to every continent, trying to develop better vegetation.

A few years ago, a movie called *It Was a Beautiful Day* came out. It was about the parents of the filmmaker, who lived on a farm in the same part of the country where I grew up. Walter and I went to see this film, and we relished the images that were so recognizable to us. We loved to hear our dialect, and we recognized every pitchfork, every rusty, patched-up wheelbarrow. We saw images of the farmer setting the remaining straw on fire after the harvest. And that's when it happened: Suddenly I had the unmistakable smell of burning straw in my nose. It was so real that I jumped up, and for a second, thought that there was a real fire.

The human mind can sometimes render a memory with such overwhelming intensity that a real physical sensation is caused by it. That's exactly what happens with a withdrawal pang. The situation, in which it occurs, always reminds you a lot of an earlier situation, in which you used to smoke. There are almost always other smokers surrounding you. And there it suddenly is, the withdrawal pang. It gives you a terrible fright: Without no trouble, you've been smoke-free for days or weeks already, you were so happy to kick the habit, and now this.

But nothing is the matter! The reason that you don't feel good during the seconds the withdrawal lasts is that you also felt miserable while you were smoking, when you were still addicted. Don't make the mistake of thinking that it's really the cigarette that you miss. It is only a short and strong memory of the past. If it happens to you, don't do anything at all. Just realize what a horrible addiction it was that you got rid of, and that you are experiencing a final after-shock. And be assured that these withdrawal pangs are rare and that they will become more and more rare. I have experienced four or five of them at the most, all during the first three months after quitting. The first time, let it spoil a nice evening. But even then, I didn't feel tempted to actually light a cigarette. I knew that I didn't want that, because I was way too happy about not being addicted anymore. But during the withdrawal pain itself, it seems for a moment that you will keep missing this lousy act of smoking for the rest of your life. For me, that created a horrible feeling that I could not shake for the rest of the evening.

The next day, the sun was shining again, and the evening before just seemed like a bad dream. With the withdrawal pang, it is the same, as a matter of fact. It is a very short and very bad daydream about an addiction that is already over. After that first one, I had a few more of those withdrawal pangs. I just looked at each one and said to myself, "Wow, that was a heavy pang! What an incredibly horrible addiction it was that I got out of." And within ten seconds, each one was over.

As withdrawal pangs are responsible for large "Difficult Moments" once in a while, so you will also have some small "difficult moments" caused by something else. These moments actually aren't caused by quitting smoking, for they are the difficult moments that everybody has once in a while, addicted or not. It's just that as an addict, you are used to lighting a cigarette for every difficult moment. You can make yourself believe that it will get a little bit less difficult if you do that. In the beginning of this book, I explained why this is not true. Still, you will have to get used to the fact that you won't have your fake support system anymore in a difficult moment. I will give an example.

The other day, I went out to dinner with a friend. I didn't know him so well yet, but he's a nice guy, and I would like it if we became closer friends. We sit down at our table and look around a little bit. At that time, I have a small difficult moment. It seems as if I miss the cigarette. But actually, it is something else altogether. I want to make smart conversation and for a moment I don't know what to say. The conversation hangs, and I feel insecure. Half a minute later, the conversation goes on again, and we have a very pleasant evening, during which I don't miss smoking for a second.

Every human being has these little difficult moments. They are moments in which you feel inhibited, sometimes a little frustrated or insecure. They could also be moments in which you want to shelter yourself behind an image or want to impress somebody else. In all these situations, you have a negative judgment about yourself. There are two ways to react to these small difficult moments. You can hate them and think you are weak, because you miss smoking for a second. That will start up the old addiction machine. That's what changes a small difficult moment into a difficult evening. After one or more difficult evenings, you will start smoking again. After which you will still have those small difficult moments, by the way, but now accompanied by a difficult addiction.

You can also react in the right way. Accept that you sometimes have little difficult moments. It is very normal to feel insecure once in a while. It is very natural to want to shelter behind an image from time to time. Just stop giving yourself a hard time for having a hard time.

Nowadays, if I find myself in a situation in which the conversation hangs for a moment, I just let it happen. What's wrong with some silence? Talking becomes a lot easier too, if silence is no longer forbidden.

Are you in a certain situation in which you suddenly have to think of smoking? Let that thought be and try to figure out why you feel insecure in that situation. Are you hiding something? Are you staging an act? Are you afraid that the other person won't like you? Are you angry at yourself for feeling insecure? As soon as you consider yourself in a loving and honest way, the thought of smoking will disappear. Besides, don't you agree that it's a charming and attractive trait in other people if they show some insecurity and look a little vulnerable? That's how charming you could be when you are having a brief difficult moment. You don't need to be shrouded in smoke anymore.

Chapter 36

Gaining Weight?

Thinking about quitting smoking, one of my biggest fears was gaining weight. During the previous attempt to quit, I had gained eighteen pounds in four weeks, and I was scared that this would happen again. When I finally quit anyway (so now according to the Free Yourself Method), I only gained about seventeen ounces in three months! Why did I gain eighteen pounds with the previous attempt to quit, whereas this time it was only a few ounces? The difference is caused by a lack of frustration through the Free Yourself Method. I will explain this.

There are different causes for gaining weight after quitting smoking. The first cause is a purely biological one: By quitting smoking, a light change in your metabolism will occur. Because of this, you may gain between a half and a whole percent of your original weight. So for the average adult of 160 pounds it can never be more than 1 pound and 4 ounces, but mostly a lot less. This gain in weight is, in fact, negligible. All other weight gain is caused by an increase in eating and snacking. If a person quits smoking the traditional way, he will become highly frustrated with the battle that he goes himself into. For in that case, you have to tell yourself dozens of times a day I AM NOT ALLOWED TO SMOKE. That will result in the constant feeling that you have to miss a goody all the time. That will give you a feeling of enormous frustration. And frustration demands compensation. Every time you feel the missing of a cigarette, you will grab a cookie, candy, pastry, or whatever.

Every smoker knows that the first cigarette after a warm meal tastes very good. This is because the warm and salty meal you just ate has lubricated your throat so the burning feeling that is usually in your throat and the taste of smoke in your mouth have disappeared for a while. This one after-dinner cigarette is sometimes so important to the smoker, that he will eat his dinner as fast as possible, just to be able to smoke that cigarette as soon as possible. It seems as if you eat only in order to be able to smoke again.

If you quit smoking in the traditional way, you will keep longing for a cigarette, especially that cigarette after dinner. During dinner, you already start dreading the end of it a little bit, because you know that you will get into this fight with yourself about that cigarette. And what happens when you dread something? You postpone it. So you will postpone the end of dinner a little. You help yourself to some more, although you are not hungry anymore. Lingering at the dinner table, you take another potato or carrot from the tray. You put more work into dessert. And when the difficult moment is finally there, with the coffee, you take some chocolate and a liqueur. Of course, in this way you will very quickly gain weight.

If you quit smoking in the traditional way, you only quit lighting cigarettes, while in your head you go on being addicted to smoking. Because of this addiction you tell yourself dozens of times a day that you are not allowed to smoke, and that you are pitiful and deserve a goody. That's why you start eating, but you feel very well that this eating is compulsive somehow. It won't take long before you start feeling guilty about stuffing yourself. This guilt is not a pleasant feeling, so you need to be comforted even more, by some ice cream, or some chocolate, or a big dinner. After which you will feel even more guilt. You are angry with yourself and see yourself as a weakling. These feelings will probably sound familiar to you. They are the characteristic traits of addiction. You have quit smoking, but your addiction is still there and manifests itself in eating sweets and food—a typical case of 'from the frying pan into the fire.'

If you quit using the Free Yourself Method, you will break your addiction before you actually stop lighting cigarettes, so you won't gain more weight than those few ounces caused by the change in your metabolism. For instead of feeling any frustrations about missing something good, you will feel strength and independence, because you will no longer feel the urge to do something that you don't agree with. I have even seen people at the Free Yourself training session, who decided to quit smoking and at the same time started losing weight. Especially during those first weeks after quitting, you feel fantastic about your new freedom and independence. It gives you the feeling that you are in control of other aspects of your life as well. When you are enjoying this feeling, it is very well possible to change your eating habits if you feel like it. If you do, you heighten your sense of power and freedom, and you can start solving other problems. Quitting smoking is for many people a landmark, indicating a major turning point in their lives: from victim of circumstances to director of your own life.

So quitting smoking can be of considerable consequence to your consuming behavior. It's advisable to keep an eye on this effect, for there is a risk that you will start to avoid certain things. For example: If you are afraid of having a drink, because you fear that you will want a cigarette with it, then have that drink. The same goes for coffee. If you really feel like drinking it, then don't avoid that confrontation. Maybe you will even truly enjoy that coffee for the first time in your life, knowing that you don't have to smoke with it anymore.

But it could very well be that you don't really feel like having that drink or that (third, fourth, and fifth cup of) coffee. You used to need that drink or that coffee, because otherwise cigarettes tasted bad. When I still smoked, I drank several glasses of port wine every evening. I thought I needed them in order to sleep well at night. The truth is that I needed that alcohol to lubricate and stimulate my throat a little, so that I could still smoke the twentieth to the thirtieth cigarette of the day. After quitting smoking, those glasses of port quietly disappeared from my menu. I still sleep very well.

It's important not to let the joy of quitting be spoiled by the fear of gaining weight in the first days after quitting. Make sure you have a lot of fruit in the house. Also, drink a lot of water. With every apple you eat and with every glass of water you drink, feel that you are helping the big clean-up inside of you, and realize that you will be free of nicotine within several days. I had also bought a little bag of sugar-free candies, as a preparation for difficult moments. It took me over three weeks to finish it.

Don't worry too much about your weight during those first weeks. If you can't refrain from consulting the scales, then don't get nervous if you did gain three or four pounds. By all means, don't get mad at yourself. If you really think that the weight you gained is not acceptable, then do something about it. Don't start this masochism of no cookie with the tea, or no ketchup with your French fries. Deal with the weight problem in the same way that you dealt with the smoking problem—positively, relentlessly, and permanently.

If you quit smoking using the Free Yourself Method, you'll only gain a tiny bit of weight. In addition, you can adjust your consuming behavior in a direction that suits you best. Still, it's important not to be afraid of this small weight gain of in advance. Some ex-smokers will let their addiction in through the back door again, because of their fear of gaining weight. Unconsciously, they will start snacking and eating a lot, in order to be able to say after a few weeks that this is going too far. "I'd rather be a thin smoker than a fat non-smoker" is the reason they give for starting to smoke again. As if smoking were a free choice here! As if it were impossible to be slender when you don't smoke! As if it were some sort of disaster to gain a few pounds. The addict will try to think of any excuse in order to legitimize smoking. It would be better to think, "I'd rather feel strong and healthy with a few extra pounds than weak, filthy and unhealthy with a few pounds less."

If you quit smoking on the condition that you won't gain any weight, you will have a difficult time, and you will probably gain weight. Quitting smoking is something you do unconditionally, because you don't want to suffocate yourself anymore with this oppressive and lethal addiction. If you quit in this way, chances are you will hardly gain any weight at all. If you gain some weight anyway, then that's a new situation that is independent of your former smoke addiction. You can just make a choice again: Accept the gained weight, or do something about it. To start smoking again in order to lose weight is the same as killing a mosquito on your forehead with a brick. To keep smoking out of fear of gaining weight is the same as letting your house burn to the ground, because the fire extinguisher will wet the carpet.

Indeed, an addiction is comparable to a smoldering house fire that slowly destroys your body and breaks down your confidence little by little. As long as you don't extinguish that fire, you will always keep feeling guilty and weak. Plus, the risk will remain that this smoldering house fire will turn into a blazing fire that will completely destroy you. But you can extinguish this fire, totally and permanently, in just one day, in one instant even. The fear that you experience when you think about it will disappear the moment you make the definitive decision. After that, there is only relief, independence, health, energy, and happiness. Can you already start feeling it? Wait a little longer. Read on first. Smoke another cigarette if you feel like it. It doesn't matter anymore, you're almost done with smoking now.

Chapter 37

The Life Crisis

It can happen to anybody: your relationship comes to an end; the job you really wanted is given to someone else; somebody you love dies; you lose your job; your child gets seriously ill. In short, you're facing a crisis situation. During such a crisis, there is a greater chance of sliding back into an addiction. I will give you an example.

The other day I ran into an old friend, whom I will call Agnes for now. We hadn't seen each other for about four years and went for a drink. When we sat down, Agnes lit a cigarette right away. I knew that she had quit smoking years ago. I asked her about it, and she told me that she had started smoking an occasional cigarette a few weeks ago. And then the whole story came out. After three years of living together, her boyfriend left in the meanest possible way. It was not just splitting up, which can be hard enough, no it was really a case of being cheated on, finding out, being robbed, being dumped, and becoming homeless! We talked for a couple of hours; we were having a good time, and at the end I asked her why she hadn't smoked any more cigarettes during our whole talk, besides that first one. She laughed, "Oh, I must have forgotten about it," and lit one up immediately. When I asked her why she had started again, she said, "I'm in so much trouble, they can all go to hell. I think I deserve a little treat now." She had a short coughing fit after the first puff, a guilty smile, and the apology, "I only smoke about five a day."

Agnes had found herself in a life crisis and started smoking again. She was having such a hard time, and she felt that she should pamper herself for now. Notice the phrase "for now," with which she indicates that it's absolutely not her intention to keep smoking forever. The idea is that it is a temporary indulgence. Hasn't she already proved that she is able to quit? She just chooses to do what she likes, for now. That's how she argues.

What we see here is the surface that hides the addiction trap. The surface consists of the misconception that smoking was a good thing and that you did give yourself a treat with it. The remarkable thing in Agnes's case is that she even had to make an effort to become addicted again. She didn't enjoy smoking at all yet, and during our intensive conversation, she even forgot about it. Still, she showed some consciousness of the negative sides of smoking, by smiling that guilty smile and by saying that she only smoked five a day.

Hidden below this surface is a deeper trap. Agnes was not only sad and angry, but she also hated herself a lot. For years, she had had the feeling that her boyfriend wasn't honest with her, that he didn't speak his mind, and that he often put her down. But she wanted this relationship to go on so badly that she worked on restoring the peace time and again. What a stupid fool she had been! Like a naive, dependent teenager, she had been outwitted and misled. And the most frustrating part was that she even missed the asshole. Agnes hated herself for that.

With a life crisis, under the surface of sadness and loneliness, there is a deeper level of self-hatred: feelings of guilt, self-reproach, powerlessness, and resistance. This self-hatred generates the need to torture and destroy oneself. The addiction is an ideal means to this end. For take a good look: In a life crisis, the need for self-destruction is disguised as self-pity. The addiction offers this self-destruction, disguised as pampering. Demand and supply are in perfect balance here. Or, as the Chinese proverb says, "The smell of fried fish will be paid for with the sound of chinking coins." The self-hatred disguised as self-pity is satisfied by self-destruction disguised as self-indulgence.

With certain problems, you dislike yourself and this means that you—usually unconsciously—want to punish yourself. It often happens in a life crisis, that you want to destroy yourself out of self-hatred. When people have this feeling, they will often get this "they-can-all-go-to-hell-now-but-I-will-do-as-I-please" feeling. In fact, you tell yourself to go to hell at such a time. It is your deeper sense of warmth and care for yourself that is smashed to pieces at such a "they-can-go-to-hell" moment.

The most radical form of self-destruction is suicide. The rope, the train, the high building and the overdose are the most frequently used methods. Most of us will have a lot of problems with these methods though: the fear of death, the love for some people close to us, the urge to live, the taboo on suicide by our religion. Besides, this "solution" misses its goal: When you are dead, you are no longer able to express your self-hatred.

That's why addiction is an attractive alternative. It satisfies the need to destroy yourself slowly, while you can still tell yourself that it's not such a bad thing, and that you could use a little treat in these miserable circumstances. This creeping kind of self-destruction has another effect as well: Not only does it destroy your health, but also your psychological integrity. Because of the addiction, you will have the chance to feel that you're a weakling dozens of times a day, to feel guilty and hateful towards yourself. These addiction feelings agree perfectly with the feelings belonging to a life crisis. Look at Agnes's case. She felt she was weak for not getting out of that relationship sooner. She hated herself for missing the man who had treated her so badly. So she felt a need for something that would make her feel weak as well, that would make her hate herself as well. That is the need for self-destruction. She felt the need to smoke! Or, better put, she needed an addiction to express her need to destroy herself. At the start, she had to put some effort into smoking these cigarettes, because they were filthy. But she remembered that smoking had once tasted good, and that it had been a support in difficult times. So she kept trying to enjoy those cigarettes.

A serious loss or rejection can turn into a life crisis. But the crisis will only turn into self-destruction by the self-rejection that is joined to it. It is not the grief or loneliness itself that gets you into a crisis, but your reaction to your grief and loneliness. You are blaming yourself for being sad. You feel guilty about your wrecked relationship. You think you are stupid for losing your job. You think it is so sad that you are sad. On top of that, you try very hard to push away these bad feelings of sadness and loneliness. Sometimes you temporarily succeed, but these pushed-away feelings will always return stronger than they were before. It is actually you who are making an immense pile of misery by shoving forward the original—and completely natural—grief.

Why do we actually hate these feelings of grief and loneliness so much and why do we hate ourselves if we get these feelings? That is passed on to us during the first five years of our lives. I sometimes call it the psychological equivalent of what in Christianity is called "original sin." For how many parents have learned to express their feelings, bad feelings in particular? How often have you seen your parents cry when you were little? And how did your father react to the crying of your mother? During the first years of childhood, almost everybody is trained to push away grief and pain and to tie these feelings to self-reproach and guilt.

What steps should you take when you find yourself in a life crisis, in order not to fall back into the smoking addiction? The fact that you know this psychological mechanism now will certainly help you. If you get the idea of pampering yourself with a cigarette when you find yourself in a crisis situation, you know now that that would be fooling yourself. You will know that it is a consequence of the urge to destroy yourself that belongs to every crisis. So you will be able to tell yourself, "I have enough problems at the moment. I don't need to add the problems of a smoke addiction to that." For that crisis will be over in several weeks or months, but it will probably take years to get rid of that addiction again.

Then you can start looking for ways to truly give yourself a treat. Take an extra holiday. Or finally usher in a change in your house that you have been planning for such a long time already. Another way to truly give yourself something is to look at your mistake in order to avoid it in the future. Agnes could learn from her broken relationship that you can never ignore your own feelings without getting punished, and that—in future relationships—she shouldn't swallow her doubts and criticism out of fear of rejection.

See, it is possible to be critical about yourself without self-reproach. There is a great saying: "To err is human." We human beings make mistakes. In that, we prove to be human. You can think you are stupid or hate yourself for making those mistakes. In that case, you will probably make those mistakes a lot more often. You can also accept your mistakes as a sign of your humanity and learn from them. Now that is truly giving yourself a treat.

Finally, you can give yourself a treat by imagining how you would support your best friend in such hard times. Or how you would support your own child. Why shouldn't you be equally warm and understanding towards yourself? You don't have to stay imprisoned in that cycle of self-reproach and self-destruction. There are no laws, not even psychological ones, that say you have to stay the way your parents raised you. You can step out of it and start a new cycle, one of self-love and self-development. Quitting smoking is a very effective way of turning the negative spiral into a positive one. From my own experience and a lot of others who have used the Free Yourself Method, I know that your life becomes really fulfilling if you quit blocking yourself emotionally, if you quit slowly destroying yourself and start to really enjoy. Isn't that something you've already wanted for years and have been afraid of for all that time? That fear only goes away after you have taken the big step. You already know that you are going to take it very soon. This opportunity is too seductive for you, too challenging, too promising, to let it go just like that. A little longer...

Chapter 38

Attempt or Decision

So what is the secret of the Free Yourself Method? How is it possible that it makes you quit smoking and that you won't feel the urge to smoke anymore, from day one? The secret consists of several secrets. Actually, they are no secrets. The method just consists of several parts that are put together for the first time.

The first part of the method shows that smoking doesn't do anything positive for you, that it only gives you withdrawal. Every cigarette removes the withdrawal, but also creates a new, future withdrawal. By removing the withdrawal, it seems as if the cigarette tastes good sometimes, or as if it helps to fight stress and boredom, or helps to concentrate or relax. The truth is that smoking heightens stress and boredom, and that it hinders concentration and relaxation.

The Free Yourself Method also explains what an addiction is. It is a psychological trap—a trap that makes you the prisoner of all kinds of negative emotions: fear of a terrible disease and feelings of guilt for keeping smoking anyway. You feel you are weak for smoking, when you don't even feel like it. You feel dependent and trapped, because of that compulsion to smoke. You are ashamed when other people are bothered by your smoke. And you develop a self-cynicism when you realize how much money you spend on this destructive addiction.

The Free Yourself Method shows that on a deeper level, the smoke addiction fulfills an unconscious need for self-destruction. When your life is in a crisis, this need becomes stronger. The added disadvantage of an addiction is that it keeps it self alive, even when a life crisis is over. After a while, it becomes unclear if you smoke because you are in a crisis situation, or if you keep having a crisis feeling because of the smoking. What is clear is that the crisis situation will get worse and will take longer if you start smoking when you're in it.

The Free Yourself Method shows that a double fear arises as soon as you start thinking about quitting. On the one hand, there is the fear that you won't succeed, which would make you condemn yourself as a weakling. On the other hand, there is the fear that you will succeed, so that you will miss smoking for the rest of your life and your life will be boring and empty. Both fears are typical features of the addiction. Both fears will cease to exist, as soon as you get out of the addiction for good. From that moment on, the fear will change into relief and a strong feeling of independence and self-respect.

It is very important with this to understand the difference between an attempt and a decision. An attempt is conditional. When you are making an attempt to quit, you tell yourself, "I will try to quit smoking, but if it becomes too hard, I'll start again." Failure is innate in the attempt, and you will already try to cover yourself for this failure. With an attempt, you already foresee that it will be extremely hard. That fear belongs to the addiction. In short, with an attempt, you take the addiction with you, and quitting can become very difficult indeed. Making an attempt seems to be less scary than making a decision. However, with an attempt, the difficulties will start right after quitting; whereas with a decision, the most difficult part comes before the quitting, namely in deciding upon the decision itself. After that, quitting is no problem anymore.

Imagine a friend telling you, "Yesterday I tried to make a nice Tibetan pizza." You would already know that it was not a success. If it had been a success, he would have said, "Yesterday I made a nice Tibetan pizza."

Imagine this friend telling you, "I have tried to quit smoking." You already know that he still smokes. In fact, the attempt to quit belongs to the addiction. How often haven't you tried to smoke a little less, to postpone the next cigarette, or not to smoke in certain situations? All those attempts will only result in a stronger need for a cigarette, and will heighten the compulsion of smoking. All this trying also gives you a stronger feeling of guilt, or a stronger feeling of "I'm so weak."

And now you want to make an attempt again not to smoke anymore? Oh, stop this trying! You already did it so often, this trying. Making an attempt is one of the final and meanest tricks of the addiction, focused on making you feel even worse and even weaker. Don't torture yourself any longer with this miserable smoke addiction! Stop trying! Make a decision!

A decision is the opposite of an attempt. An attempt takes the path of failure, whereas a decision not only takes the line of success, but the decision in itself is already a success. An attempt is the beginning of a row of laborious change. A decision comes at the end of a laborious (inner) change, and at the beginning of evident outer change. With a decision, you definitely close a chapter of your life. A decision is taken with your whole being, with your heart and your intellect.

Your intellect says, "Smoking doesn't actually do anything. It doesn't help me in any way. It only creates an illusion, and in the meantime, it destroys me, physically as well as psychologically, and it costs a lot of money on top of that."

Your heart says, "I really don't like myself if I keep smoking. I have had enough of this fear that I can't live without cigarettes. I would like to feel fit, healthy and energetic."

Bring your life into harmony with your heart and your mind. Don't let fear mislead you. This fear only tells you that you are on the verge of an important decision in your life. If you keep smoking, this fear will diminish a little bit, true, but it will always keep playing a role in the background. Do you really want to be freed from that fear? Then you'll have to get out of the addiction.

Are you still doubting? Are you still weighing the advantages against the disadvantages? Then read some chapters again. The so-called advantages of smoking only exist in the eyes of the addict. They seem to be advantages as long as you are still addicted. For someone who is not addicted, there are no advantages in smoking. For someone who is not addicted, there are only disadvantages in smoking. Realize that it's not about smoking or not smoking here. The choice is between being addicted or not being addicted.

It might seem as if there is a third choice, namely not choosing at all, or putting off the choice. With addictions, however, not choosing equals choosing the addiction. In fact, not choosing and postponing are traits of the addiction. Be honest, for almost the whole time that you are smoking now, you are postponing quitting.

Before you undertake a decision, consider seriously the opposite of the decision: What will happen if I keep smoking? There has been one woman in my training session, who decided to keep smoking afterwards. It was truly a conscious decision, and she told me later that she had actually enjoyed smoking for several weeks. After those weeks, of course, the old feelings of guilt came back again. You can't go on forever making yourself believe that you are addicted out of your own free will. Several weeks later, she quit smoking.

Ask yourself what the advantages are of deciding to keep smoking. Try to see clearly that keeping smoking means staying addicted. And that you will always be imprisoned in that mediocrity, in that half-heartedness, in all those negative feelings about yourself. You see, the most essential question that you have to ask yourself is: Do you want to escape from that addiction? Do you want to be happier than you are now? Do you feel that you are worth it?

A decision needs to be undertaken with your whole being, not just with your heart and your mind. Something else is needed. Some people call it intuition and others talk about a higher knowing or idealism. What you call it is not important. I'm talking about certain values that you would like to express in your life. A value is not the same as a feeling. Independence would for instance be such a value. It is not something that you constantly feel, but whenever your independence is in jeopardy, you might feel unhappy. Freedom is another one of those values. Love, health, honesty, integrity—they are all values. Examine which values are extra important to you. Which values would you like to express in your life? Now take a look at how an addiction goes against those values. See how being addicted keeps you from actualizing the most important values in your life! And then, make your decision. Make it with your intellect. Make it with your heart. Come to your decision with your intuition, your higher knowledge, or whatever you call it, and realize that the most important values in your life are served by this decision. Make the decision unconditionally and definitively. Don't say, "I am not allowed to smoke anymore." Just say, "I don't need to destroy myself anymore, not now nor later." The way you have always felt as an addict—weak, unhealthy, and alienated from yourself—you never need to feel like that anymore.

Before making a decision, you should also take a look at the future. How will your decision influence your future? Imagine how you will look in ten, twenty, thirty years, or even longer. How will you look when the afternoon or evening of your life has come? Imagine how your face will look if you quit smoking now. How do you want to look when you are old? Do you want freedom, independence, health, and self-respect to glow from your face when you are old? It only depends on you, on the decision that you are going to make now. Do you long to be freed from your addiction? Then make that decision, for once and for all. Grant yourself that fantastic feeling to have changed your life, to have chosen for a better life, fears and all. It is so very blissful to be freed from smoking!

Chapter 39

Checklist

Here is a list with the most important matters for a successful decision to never smoke again. If some of these items are still not clear to you, read the chapters regarding those subjects again.

- Never take nicotine again, in any form.
- Smoking doesn't have anything positive to offer you, only illusions.
- Never try NOT to think of smoking. Pushing away certain thoughts will only strengthen them.
- Never tell yourself: I AM NOT ALLOWED TO SMOKE. Also never say, "I am not allowed to crave a smoke." Do say, "I don't want to be addicted anymore."

- No substitutes, such as joints, herbal cigarettes, candy, alcohol, etc. Don't try any tricks to make it "easier." It IS easy (after making the decision) and tricks will only make it harder.
- No evasion. Don't evade other smokers, or situations that you used to smoke a lot in. You will only make it harder for yourself.
- Don't ever *attempt* to quit anymore. Choose between being addicted or not, and make a *decision*.
- Whenever you are having a difficult moment, realize that smoking is the *cause* of this difficult moment, not the solution for it. Smoking is never the solution for a problem, it is only an extra problem added.
- Smoking is destroying yourself. Quitting smoking is really pampering yourself. You pamper yourself with feelings of power, freedom, and independence, with enormous extra vitality, energy, and health.
- Maybe you will have a difficult moment once in a while. Read a little in this book at such a time. Read the letter you wrote to yourself. Save both of them in a special place. Keep trusting that a difficult moment will always pass by very quickly as long as you don't start worrying.

If you follow these guidelines, nothing can go wrong. Know that you are not the first one who is quitting using this method. If others are able to quit smoking without any trouble, why wouldn't the same be true for you? They also thought that they were a lot more addicted or a lot weaker than other smokers, or that their life was a lot more difficult. They also felt enormous relief from the first day of quitting, to be freed from this suffocating addiction.

Who knows, maybe you will also have this moment of happiness that a lot of ex-smokers experience after a while. I had it only a couple of months after quitting. It was a cold, sunny winter morning. I got on my bike and drove over the quay that I live on. Suddenly it was as if everything stopped for a moment, the trees along the road, the ships on the water. The world around me looked so light and clear. I realized that I really never had to smoke anymore. I felt intensely happy. It was an epiphany, which slowly faded after several seconds.

I don't have an explanation for this phenomenon. For also earlier, right after quitting, I had been feeling relieved and happy about not smoking anymore. Maybe this experience happens, because it takes a while after quitting, before you realize with your deepest inner self that you are truly free of the addiction. Some people have this moment of happiness several weeks after quitting, some never experience it, but are happy to have quit anyway. This moment of happiness has nothing to do with successfully quitting. But I hope you will experience it, too, as an extra gift of life to you. Because you feel that life is important enough to merit stepping out of this lethal addiction.

Chapter 40

The Last Cigarette

With quitting smoking, it is important to consciously smoke your last cigarette. You can only smoke your last cigarette after you have decided to quit smoking. Otherwise, you wouldn't be sure that it is the last one. The last cigarette is the only cigarette you smoke after deciding to quit. It is actually a symbol for that one cigarette that you will never have to smoke anymore, namely the next one. This last cigarette is also an important symbolic farewell to your addiction. Before you start smoking this last cigarette, here are some guidelines.

The most important rule is this one: There is no special way to smoke this last cigarette. You can light it, watch it for a long time and throw it away. You can smoke it until it burns your fingers. You can think it tastes filthy or extremely good. With the smoking of this cigarette, only one thing really matters—the realization that it is your last one. Smoke this cigarette consciously. Make sure that you can't be disturbed while you are at it. Let your past go by in your mind's eye and watch how important this addiction has been to you. Say good-bye without resentment, without regrets, without feeling anger or reproach, and let every feeling that you experience pass. If you still feel fear, accept it as a leftover from your old addiction. And give yourself the chance to also feel gentleness and love for yourself, to feel the integrity, independence, freedom, health, and all other values that you express with this one decision.

After the last cigarette, you are rid of smoking for good. What should you do with the remaining cigarettes? That doesn't matter at all. I made a big ceremony out of throwing all of them over the railing of my ship. My girlfriend let half a package of tobacco lie on the table for weeks after she had quit. For her, that was a symbol of freedom. Do with it whatever you like best. It doesn't matter. And congratulate yourself for ending this destructive addiction. Enjoy the regained freedom. Accept moments of insecurity. Be proud of your independence. And start looking for the next challenge. You've licked the smoking problem now. Are there any other nice things you can do in order to improve the quality of your life? Don't leave it go at this, keep on treating yourself well. Life has so much more to offer. Enjoy!

Epilogue

For People Who Want to Rid Somebody Else of Smoking

People who don't smoke, but who have a partner who does, sometimes wish that he or she would quit. That could be because of the smell in the house, the dirty ashtrays or the bad breath, but it is even more painful to see how a beloved person gets more and more entangled in self-destruction and feelings of guilt about it.

All this could lead to an actual attempt on your part to try to make your partner quit. I have to warn you though: The effect of such an attempt is usually disastrous. If you are lucky, the addict will only start smoking more. But a serious, even definite dislocation of your relationship also belongs to the possibilities. For the addict will do everything in his might to make you stop "acting so annoying about smoking." And for you the disillusion will remain that for your partner, the addiction is more important than the relationship with you. If you want to use some influence to make your partner quit anyway, you have to be very careful. Reading this book could prevent a lot of misery in this.

The general rule is that you can never make a smoker quit by pointing out the negative aspects of smoking. Every remark about damaging his health, losing fitness, ruining the atmosphere, the stinking of his breath, his clothes and the whole house, will bring him deeper into the addiction. All these remarks will feed the feelings of guilt and shame that every addict has (although some are very good at repressing these feelings). Really, smokers already know that it's destructive and unhealthy, and that it stinks, even when they deny or dismiss it.

Also every appeal to love, solidarity, or responsibility for the relationship will work in the wrong way. If you want to double the smoke production in your house, you should say something like "just do it for me," or "out of love for our children." These remarks will confront the addict with his own feelings of powerlessness. He is ashamed by his fear of quitting. He resists the idea that he has to quit, and these negative feelings have to be subdued with cigarettes again.

If you live with a smoking partner, what you can do is suggest to make certain parts of your house smoke free. Make sure that in suggesting this, you show no trace of reproach, no condemning of the smoking itself at all. The suggestion only comes out of the reasonable idea that for non-smokers, it is more pleasant to eat and sleep in smoke-free rooms. Of course, the smoker has to give his consent to this arrangement. It is possible that as compensation, he will want you to never make a remark about his smoking behavior again. Agree with this. You'll never have to say anything anymore, for after this agreement, the smoker will be confronted with his addiction on a daily basis, all by himself. Each time he has to go to another room for a cigarette, he will feel worthless. The naturalness of smoking, or doing it without thinking, is broken. In the long term, this will have a positive effect on the motivation to quit.

Finally, you could support the smoker by showing understanding and compassion with his problem of being addicted. You can ask him if he wouldn't rather be freed from that compulsion and that oppression. Point out to him that there is a method with which it can be done without any withdrawal misery. If you want to throw this book into the battle, put it somewhere in the house in a visible place. Don't ever pressure him to read it. The smoker really will have to find this moment himself. And trust this: The moment will come sooner or later.

Appendix

What Do I Do if I Am Unable to Quit Smoking Even After I Have Read the Book?

You don't have to read this part of the book before you quit smoking, only after quitting. Especially when you have the feeling that you did not "completely" succeed. In that case, the next few pages may be of use to you, because there are several degrees of failure.

1. Complete Failure

If in the first or second day after quitting, you are climbing up the walls, and you're craving a cigarette almost all of the time, you can safely assume that your "quitting" has failed. You are still addicted and are trying to use willpower not to smoke. Stop tormenting yourself and just continue to smoke for the time being, because you never actually stopped in the first place. Obviously you did not completely switch off the addiction.

Please acknowledge however that you had and still have the courage to face your addiction. Your best efforts have failed this time. So go ahead and smoke, but do so without judging yourself or wallowing in self-loathing and without dragging along feelings of stupidity or weakness. What would be helpful now is to carefully consider the effect of each cigarette you smoke. Observe precisely how you feel and ask yourself, "Why am I smoking again?" If the cigarette tastes good, enjoy it. If the cigarette tastes like shit, notice the compulsion. Just notice how you feel while smoking. In this way, you will eventually reach the point where you are ready to quit smoking again! When this happens, you could try to read this book a second time. But sometimes the effect will be less than when you read it the first time. You can also read my next book, *Beyond Addiction* (check with the publisher) to support your decision to quit again. Many smokers who have failed to quit, experience this as the ultimate proof that they are too weak to quit. In reality, every failure to stop brings you closer to the one time you will be successful and completely free yourself from smoking. So don't give up on yourself.

2. Quitting Successfully But Then Relapsing

Some people that use the Free Yourself Method to stop smoking succeed initially, but after a while fall back into addiction. The first weeks you feel great. You're glad you quit smoking, and you have no craving whatsoever for a cigarette. Then, all of a sudden, completely unexpectedly, you light one and begin smoking again. How is this possible? There are several ways this can take place. It may be that you are dreading the very first withdrawal pangs, so you immediately smoke a cigarette just to avoid that feeling. For some, the fear of experiencing withdrawal pangs is so subtle yet strong that you smoke that first cigarette before you are even aware of the compulsion.

In other cases, a kind of hubris about how easy it was for you to quit creates a dangerous fallacy. "If it is that easy to quit, I can easily smoke one every now and then" is the fallacy these people fall prey to. In truth, quitting is never easy, even using the Free Yourself Method. The aftermath is much easier with this method, but ironically, for some smokers, this is the great pitfall.

Now that you have started to smoke again, you will have to conquer your fear of stopping all over again, even after experiencing how wonderful it was to be free of smoking. That is how irrational this addiction fear is and how strong: To know that it is wonderful to be free of this addiction doesn't help conquer the fear. There is really only one way to get rid of this fear of quitting, and that is to quit. So if you start smoking again, don't condemn yourself, because "To err is human." Enjoy smoking. Register as carefully as possible what it does to you. In this way, you don't have to stay addicted very long before you reach the point of allowing yourself to step out of it again.

3. You Succeeded But Are Not Happy

Occasionally people succeed in ending their addiction, but they miss the "joy" that should come with stopping successfully. They no longer need a cigarette. There is no doubt that they have quit smoking, and there are no problems with withdrawal. Yet at the same time, they feel dejected and depressed, or a little melancholy. They know they should be pleased, but they don't feel that way. They are going through a classic grieving process. For some smokers, the cigarette was seen as a "buddy" and a "supporter" during difficult times. They have stopped smoking, because they see through this sham. In fact, this "buddy" causes the misery from which it then seems to offer consolation. Hence they are successful in leaving their addiction behind, but this grieving process can take several weeks or even months. Although your "buddy" was certainly destructive and exacting company, he or she was also very familiar.

If you are in this situation, don't fight it. Don't make the mistake of thinking that your joy of living will return if you start smoking again. It was not because of joyfulness that you stopped smoking. Ask yourself whether you have enough joyful things in your life. Maybe you lack things you can look forward to. In this respect the cigarette regularly used to offer you an object to look forward to, a regular "moment for yourself," even though this was an illusion caused by the addiction. That's why the loss of these moments can cause a feeling that life no longer has meaning. It is time for you to create new things in your life that you can look forward to—not out of compulsion, but just to do yourself a favor. That way, these "moments for yourself" will no longer be "moments against yourself" but genuinely "moments with yourself."

Sometimes the reason that you don't feel happy after successfully quitting is quite simple: You just can't believe that you are capable of such a success! Although you experience no craving, you just can't believe it is true; certainly, it has to go wrong soon. You constantly put your back against the wall, waiting for the moment the bomb of craving and yearning for a smoke is going to fall. You live in the lull before the storm, which makes you unable to enjoy your newly won freedom.

Here is only one piece of advice: Relax! This shitty-addiction is over! You're still alive! You're free again! In the next few days you can put some extra attention to the physical benefits of quitting: You breathe more air. You feel more energy and less heart beating when running up the stairs. And finally, why not explicitly acknowledge to yourself that you did it! You pulled it off! Maybe you are not as weak, stupid or bad as you always felt while being addicted. Go ahead, stand in front of a mirror and give yourself a heartfelt congratulation. I know this is a bit scary but quitting smoking is much scarier and you did that too. So now start enjoying your success!

4. Multi-Stoppers

In every Free Yourself Method training there are a few of them—the multi-stoppers. These are the people who are not afraid to quit smoking. They know in advance that they will stop smoking and enjoy it, but they also know that after a few months, when not smoking has become "business as usual", they will start smoking again. These are the yo-yo's of smoke addiction. The periods they are not smoking seem to be short vacations in the heavy job of being addicted. For these people, I especially recommend my next book *Beyond Addiction*, to discover the psychological patterns behind this self-defeating mechanism.

Other multi-stoppers are smokers who need to prove to themselves and others, once in a while, that they are not addicted. If this happens more regularly, we don't recognize them as multi-stoppers but as moderate smokers of the "I-only-smoke-when-I-want-to" type. For them, it is most important to keep up the appearance of not being an addict.

Other multi-stoppers keep on smoking until they have reached a certain level of disgust, at which point they stop rigorously and completely, until they have forgotten how disgusting it was. After a few weeks, the cycle starts again. Actually, they never stopped being addicted: Quitting has not been experienced as a victory; starting again is not seen as a failure. If you recognize this pattern in yourself, it's best to continue this cycle up to the point where the maximum disgust coincides with a sort of "meta-disgust" for this whole pattern of spinning round in this addiction. Then you will not only stop smoking, but most of all end the addiction.

5. Mopping With the Tap Open

This is a Dutch expression that means trying to solve a problem while the cause is still continuing. In this case, you stopped smoking successfully, but something else in your life is totally dysfunctional. Perhaps it is another addiction or you have a dysfunctional relationship, no job or roof above your head, no friends, no hobbies, or a combination of these factors. In this case, stopping smoking is a bit like "mopping while the tap is still open." Here we are not talking about an ordinary dip or crises situation, because quitting smoking can have a very positive influence on solving such a crisis. No, we are talking real shit here, a total disruption of your life. If this disruption is connected with several addictions, first deal with the other addictions, and only after that, end the smoking addiction.

If your life has fallen apart, ending your addictions can be a great step in the right direction, but you must also deal with the deeper causes of your problems, and ask for professional help. If, after ending your addictions, you stay in your social isolation, hanging in front of the television or playing video games all day, then it won't be long before you fall back into addiction. So, you have to plan your steps carefully. Make sure that the day you stop, you can start working with the causes of your problems, have a place to live, start therapy, find a job, etcetera. This is quite a project, but it's the only way that you will succeed in the long term in bringing back the joy in your life.

6. Finally: To Fail Successfully

Failing to quit smoking, for whatever reason, is never pleasant. There will always be feelings of failure, weakness or stupidity. When you recognize these feelings as an important part of the addiction, you no longer have to subscribe to them. You can see them as symptoms of being addicted, rather than of who you really are. By not rejecting yourself for being addicted, you can shorten the time of being addicted drastically. By acknowledging that only the addiction is filthy, not you, that it is the addiction that makes you feel weak, while you are not, by recognizing that it is your purity and strength that wants to end this terrible addiction, you can make this failure into a success. This failure will add to your conviction that addiction is not your nature, only an unfortunate and painful circumstance that brings you no happiness at all. And that, you do yourself the biggest favor of all to step out of the addiction.